D1709915

LYDIA COURTEILLE

Extraordinary Jewellery of Imagination and Dreams

LYDIA COURTEILLE

Extraordinary Jewellery of Imagination and Dreams

Juliet Weir-de La Rochefoucauld

ACC ART BOOKS

ISBN: 978 185149 837 6

British Library Cataloguing-in-Publication Data
A catalogue record for this book is available from the British Library

The author and publisher gratefully acknowledge the permission granted to reproduce the copyright material in this book. Every effort has been made to trace copyright holders and to obtain their permission for the use of copyright material. The publisher apologises for any errors or omissions in the text and would be grateful if notified of any corrections that should be incorporated in future reprints or editions of this book.

FRONTISPIECE:
'ABYSSE' COLLECTION, CROWNED SEAHORSE COUPLE PENDANT/BROOCH, c.2013 – BOULDER OPAL, SAPPHIRES (PINK, PURPLE AND BLUE), DIAMOND, BLACK RHODIUM-PLATED GOLD, WHITE GOLD

TITLE PAGE:
'QUEEN OF SHEBA' COLLECTION, SERPENT DIADEM, c.2015 – PERIDOT, TSAVORITE GARNET, YELLOW SAPPHIRE, CHAMPAGNE-COLOURED DIAMOND, BLACK RHODIUM-PLATED GOLD

---

www.antiquecollectorsclub.com
ACC Art Books
Sandy Lane, Old Martlesham, Woodbridge, Suffolk IP12 4SD, UK
Tel: 01394 389950. Email: info@antique-acc.com
or
ACC DISTRIBUTION
6 West, 18th Street, Suite 4B,New York, NY 10011, USA
Tel: 212 645 1111. Email: sales@antiquecc.com

Printed in China
for ACC Art Books Ltd., Woodbridge, Suffolk, England

CONTENTS

“ *There is no art without provocation!* ”

PREFACE

SECRET GARDEN BY DIDIER GUEDJ
PORTRAIT FOR A FRIEND

Tiger's eye, moonstone, fire opal, black or gold: gemstones which suggest a femininity are the nuances chosen by Lydia Courteille in her creative process. A traveller who losses herself in the cultures she meets, moved by the flora and fauna, her day dreams of ancient civilisations and secret unexplained thoughts are gathered together in her small notebooks.

Then the gems and nature enjoin into a fiction soon to be transformed into gold which she dresses in black. Imagination becomes reality expressed in the art of high jewellery.

Dreams and treasure come together to conspire, giving birth to incredible compositions following an unbending set of themes.

Little by little the feminine mystery unfurls, this temptress lures us assuredly into her secret garden, like a woman whispering discreetly or deliberately into the ear.

But this garden has a closed gate, a wall in each of her cherished jewels. In each jewel are the clues to her principle codes but she leaves the on-looker to create their own interpretation.

She demystifies the religious signs and icons which become simple signs of our humanity. The etymologist's world becomes playful as a starfish meets a little crab, each in their tiny bodies dressed in sapphires are heroes on a surrealist beach or in one of Lydia Courteille's dreams. Gentle, provocative, wise, aggressive, sensual, her anti-conformist mind, pushes barriers, sweeping away conventional taboos and perpetually seeks to question.

Her ode to woman's uniqueness comes alive in each of her rings, which bought by her clients, throw their sights, as if on a dress, which will shine a light upon them. Eroticism and sensuality is in reach or is worn, it is thus.

BIOGRAPHY AND BOUTIQUE

Lydia Courteille was born Liliane Schoonjans in Paris into a family that can trace its lineage back to the founders of the town Malines in Belgium. She ironically comments that the carriage transformed into a pumpkin over time.

Her family moved away from Paris before returning with her three stepsisters and her younger brother when she was eight years old. Reflecting on her home where she stayed until she was eighteen years old, she says:

> *“The fact of living in ugly grey tower blocks, makes you want to leave, to want to make something of your life.”*

Boredom is a fertile ground, on which imagination and creativity can be sown. She was an ardent reader as a child, and wrote to eighteen pen pals all over the world about her hopes and dreams, describing her lessons and the films that she saw, such as *Sissi* and *Cleopatra*; the life of a child in ’60s France. In return, she ‘travelled’ through her friends’ letters, which described their lives and which sowed the seeds for years later.

From cartoons to stamps and butterflies, Liliane’s interest jumped from one eclectic thing to another. Her room was a pot pourri of objects and creatures, books and drawings. A fan of Robert Charroux she devoured his books such as *One Hundred Thousand Years of Man’s Unknown History* (published in 1963 and as an English translation in 1970), which recounted the theory of ancient astronauts and the mysteries of the world – be it the lost city of Atlantis or the Nasca Lines. *The Dawn of Magic* by Louis Pauwels and Jacques Bergier, which related supernatural conspiracy theories was another source of wonder. She daydreamed of such legends as the valley of rubies in Burma, with eagles plunging down to grab the gemstones in their talons; the mysteries of the ‘Puerta del Sol’ in Tiahuanaco and the ovoid skulls of the ancient Mesoamerican cultures.

She was a frequent visitor to museums, especially the mineralogical museum in Paris. One moment she was a geologist collecting stones, examining her specimens under the microscope her father had given her, the next she was a fashion designer dreaming up confections of style and fashion. She invented her own worlds.

However, her first memories were of another house, on the outskirts of Lyon in Collonges-au-Mont-d’Or, the home town of the famous chef Paul Bocuse, where she lived for a short time with her family. The house belonged to Marthe Garioux, who had inherited the home from her parents, and took in paying guests.

OPPOSITE PAGE:
PORTRAIT OF LILIANE, AGED 19
Photograph by Dominique Rondoni

BELOW:
FAMILY COAT OF ARMS FOR THE SCHOONJANS FAMILY, c.1509

> *“ She welcomed my family, with four children, a cat and a dog, as lodgers. ”*

ABOVE:
LILIANE ON HOLIDAY IN FRONT OF THE EGYPTIAN PYRAMIDS
Photograph by Dominique Rondoni

TOP RIGHT:
LETTER FROM LILIANE’S JAPANESE PENPAL, WHOSE FATHER HAD POSTED IT FROM THE ASSEMBLÉE NATIONALE WHILST HE WAS ON A DIPLOMATIC MISSION TO FRANCE

RIGHT:
PENPALS SENT LILIANE POSTCARDS FROM ALL OVER THE WORLD: (CLOCKWISE FROM TOP LEFT) A FIGURE FROM THE JAIN TEMPLE, KHAJURAHO; LA PAZ, MEXICO; AND SHEIKH CHISHTI'S TOMB IN FATENPUR SIKRI IN INDIA

Marthe Garioux was a teacher at the school of fine art in Oran; her house was a treasure trove filled with curiosities: silver snuff boxes, busts in plaster and terracotta and needlework samplers.

"Her home was like a museum."

Madame Garioux had kept every edition of *La Semaine de Suzette*, from 1905 when it was first published. This weekly magazine printed illustrated stories, plays and poetry for young girls and the young Liliane plunged into its cartoons of Bécassine and Bleuette.

Just by living in this home and watching Madame Garioux give needlework lessons to the wealthy ladies who came to the house, Liliane grew up aware of the past and its inherent beauty. Each tapestry had a story to tell, in particular *The Lady and the Unicorn (La Dame à La Licorne)* from the Musée de Cluny; they were witnesses to lives gone by and that was enough for Liliane to start dreaming and conjuring up her own stories.

Marthe Garioux happened to be the daughter of a doctor and some of her father's medical books from his student days, especially those on anatomy with paper cut-out skeletons and pop-up cardboard images, found their way to the basement of her picturesque house in Collonges-au-Mont-d'Or. They were yet another temptation for the endless curiosity

ABOVE:
LILIANE SCHOONJANS (2ND FROM THE RIGHT) WITH HER MOTHER JANINE, HER SISTERS THERESE AND JACQUELINE, HER BROTHER RAYMOND AND THE FAMILY DOG

BELOW:
MARTHE GARIOUX WITH SCULPTOR FRIEND M. CHAPUIS FROM COLLONGES-AU-MONT-D'OR

of this little girl; was this the start of Liliane's fascination with science and from science to their symbolism in art? Even she cannot say for sure, but there is no denying that unconsciously or otherwise she was later to weave all these threads together to create her own fascinating world of jewellery.

When Liliane was 15 years old she travelled with her class to the great lakes in the north of Italy and it was here that, for the first time, she truly began to understand what luxury meant. She was in awe of the great palaces she saw dotted on the shores of the lakes, their terraces and immaculately kept gardens sloping gently down to the water's edge.

Later when Liliane was 16 years old, she joined a photographic club; she dreamed of being a fashion model, alas it was not to be, but she did model for her friends. Coincidence perhaps, but one too strong not to mention here, a photograph from this period shows Liliane posing with a skull; she was already thinking about the brief transitory nature of beauty and the remorseless passage of time.

OPPOSITE PAGE, TOP:
LILIANE SCHOONJANS WITH HER ELDER SISTER JACQUELINE

OPPOSITE PAGE, BOTTOM:
ADOLESCENCE – AT A TIME WHEN LILIANE SCHOONJANS WAS THINKING OF STUDYING MEDICINE

LEFT:
DETAIL FROM 'SIGHT', ONE OF THE SIX SCENES IN THE FLANDERS TAPESTRY SERIES,*THE LADY AND THE UNICORN (LA DAME À LA LICORNE)*, c.1500 – A MEMORY FROM MARTHE GARIOUX'S NEEDLEWORK CLASSES

Science was her true passion, at one point she considered medicine, eventually choosing to read biochemistry at the 'Ecole de Chimie' (School of Chemistry), Paris. She graduated with a double degree in Haematology under the great haematologist Jean Bernard at Hôtel Dieu and one in Cytology from the United States, and remained in the scientific world for ten years. It was by sheer chance that Liliane moved from this career to that of jewellery designer in the world of fine art. Reflecting on the great work by the Nobel Laureate and molecular biologist Jacques Monod, *Chance and Necessity*, she says:

> “*My life is made up of so many chance moments, most of which can be put down more to chance than to design.*”

She was to marry a photographer, Dominique Rondoni in 1973 and it was through his world that she was introduced to the golden number and painting. She learned to understand and to interpret these vestiges from the past.

THAT PESKY WATCH

In 1979, Liliane bought an art deco wristwatch that she was determined to wear, unfortunately it dropped into a puddle and from that moment it was never the same; no sooner than it was repaired than it would stop working again. A frustrated Liliane thus spent more time than she had anticipated going back and forth to the antique shop on rue Cambon, to get it repaired. The shop sold many antique pieces including cameos and 18th-century matching jewellery sets or parures. Fascinated by their splendour as she waited for her watch, Liliane was soon an expert in her own right.

"Antique jewellery from the 16th to the 20th century, ... I developed a mental dictionary of jewels. I think being around these very old pieces was a trigger for my creativity. It made me see the political side of jewellery, that it can communicate a message as well as being very pretty."

Could it have been destiny that made her buy the wristwatch? We shall never know, but it was certainly the catalyst that led Liliane to choose a different career.

Liliane would spend her weekends at the flea market and slowly but surely she began to collect these old cameos and glyptics. Marvelling at the craftsmanship that was required to create such delicate and detailed carvings, she transformed these unloved examples of extraordinary workmanship from brooches into massive rings. These were her first tentative steps as a designer: the cameos were remounted within decorative and flamboyant frameworks of enamel, gemstones and, above all, colour. They were saved, given a new lease of life, a second coming so to speak.

Liliane decided that this was to be her path and from 1981 to 1986 she enrolled herself to study gemmology to gain a deeper knowledge of gemstones.

THE CREATION OF 'LYDIA COURTEILLE'

In 1987, after several years working with the antique shop Au Vase de Delft on rue Cambon, Liliane embarked on her career as an independent antique dealer. Along with the new career came a new name: Lydia Courteille. Liliane chose this as her brand name for several reasons. 'Lydia' – as well as sounding not too dissimilar to Liliane – was the ancient nation ruled over by Croesus (595BC-c.546BC), the last king of the Mermnade line. Croesus was reputed to be extremely wealthy and to have issued the first standardised gold coins. His name is synonymous with wealth in both the ancient Greek and Persian cultures. 'Courteille' was Liliane's mother's maiden name. Slowly but surely she started to create her own jewels, starting with her cameos, or as she calls them, her '*Habillage*' (dressed) jewels. Her instinctual eye 'discovered' the jewels of Suzanne Belperron without even knowing who this great designer was, she began buying Belperron pieces and jewels from the Art Deco period. She joined the Alliance

Européenne des Experts (European Experts Alliance) in 1991, and after many years she was nominated as expert for the admissions commission for antique jewellery and gemstones for many of the important shows that take place in Paris, including the annual PAD exhibition (the Pavilion of Arts and Design in Paris).

The location of her first boutique was the Rue Duphot, just beside the Madeleine Church and within the Parisian golden triangle of luxury and couture; it happened to be at the back of Chanel Inc. so as luck would have it, she had a steady stream of initiated clients sensitive to her taste. 18th- and 19th-century parures and art deco jewellery were displayed in the window side-by-side with her new creations. They surprised more than one passerby with their size and proportions,

> *"Many people confuse big with style."*

However, they soon began to appeal to a certain type of clientele...

"I design for people who have a taste for the extravagant, who have emotion, for people who are confident in their own choices. I love to see a very classical woman come to my shop and buy an eccentric piece. It's like a code – those who don't know think that it is a fake, in a way they are testing their friends without overtly showing their wealth."

ABOVE LEFT:
CAMEO 'HABILLAGE' RING, c.2005 – 19TH-CENTURY GREEN AND BROWN JASPER CAMEO, RUBY, DIAMOND, YELLOW GOLD

ABOVE RIGHT:
CAMEO 'HABILLAGE' RING, PORTRAIT OF CATHERINE THE GREAT, c.2007 – 19TH-CENTURY CARNELIAN CAMEO, RUBY, SHELL, YELLOW AND WHITE DIAMOND, YELLOW AND WHITE GOLD

THE SÈVRES 'MEDALLION' PORCELAIN CUP AND SAUCER THAT THE YOUNG LILIANE SCHOONJANS GAVE AS A GIFT TO HER MOTHER

In 1993 Lydia Courteille set up shop in rue Saint Honoré. She now had two boutiques, which she kept for a short while. With each move, she maintained a constant in these small worlds of fantasy: her favourite colour, a deep rich Majorelle blue similar to the blue of Yves Saint Laurent's home in Marrakesh.

It was a colour that had accompanied her throughout her childhood: when she was just two years old, her father took her to a flea market in Lyons to choose a present for her mother. She chose an electric blue medallion cup and saucer in Sèvres porcelain.

"Years later I bought a suit in electric blue, a Saint Laurent blue and each time I wore the suit I would always wear a piece of jewellery with it and I found that the jewel was twice as beautiful as it was on its own. I decided that if ever I should have a boutique, it would be blue and black. My mother gave me back the cup recently, I had completely forgotten about it and it was she who recounted the story to me."

In 2002, Courteille opened a small gallery on Paris' famous Left Bank dedicated to showcasing artist jewellers, such as Line Vautrin, Jean Després and Man Ray.

> *Paris is a huge museum of the past – a kind of curiosity cabinet.*

THE JARDIN MAJORELLE, MARRAKESH, DESIGNED BY PAINTER JACQUES MAJORELLE IN 1937 AND RESTORED BY YVES SAINT LAURENT AND PIERRE BERGÉ IN THE EIGHTIES

On rue Saint Honoré, her boutique, 'Paris's best kept secret', invites us to enter into a magical world; a sophisticated unexpected world of fantasy and rebellious desire; of dreams and castles in the sky. Always in Majorelle and Castaing* blue and black, glass vitrines and black wood trellis walls, this is Lydia Courteille's 'secret garden', where gold four- leaf clovers grow alongside her special gardens of rare and unusual gemstones, each transformed into a treasure of colour, light and history to become intriguing works of art to be coveted by those who step over the threshold and into her universe.

* Madeleine Castaing was an antique collector, dealer and interior designer; she was also a great supporter of artists from the 1930s onwards. She had a huge influence on Courteille from an early point in her career. The Castaing blue – somewhere between duck egg blue and pale turquoise – was conceived to contrast the off-whites and blacks that typically appeared in her interiors; it was a blue that Courteille was determined to use where she could.

OLD INTERIOR OF LYDIA'S BOUTIQUE – NOTE THE CHANDELIER: EACH LIGHT BULB IS SUPPORTED BY MONKEYS WHO SEE, HEAR AND SPEAK NO EVIL. THE MIRROR IN THE FOREGROUND, TO THE LEFT OF THE IMAGE, IS DECORATED WITH *MEMENTO MORI*, WHILST THE PAGODA-LIKE DISPLAY CASES ARE DRESSED WITH CORAL BRANCHES AND VANITAS JEWELLERY

OPPOSITE PAGE:
FIRST PUBLICITY FOR LYDIA COURTEILLE PLACED WITH *VOGUE* ITALY, c.1998
The advertisement was offered by *Vogue* Italy to Courteille after a mishap with one of her jewels on a fashion photo shoot.

BELOW:
A SELECTION OF PRESS CUTTINGS FROM LYDIA COURTEILLE'S PRESSBOOK

THE PRESS

From the moment that Courteille first opened her first shop in 1987, *Madame Figaro* and *Vogue Italy*, followed quickly by *Vogue France,* have been constant enthusiasts of her work and she has been advertising with them since the beginning of her adventure.

Laurence Mouillefarine and Marie-Dominique Sassin (*Madame Figaro*), Nicoletta Santoro and Anna Dello Russo (*Vogue Italy*), Franceline Prat and Françoise Guittard (*Vogue France*), and Laurence Benaïm (*Stiletto France*) are just a few of the journalists who have showcased Courteille's artistic talent in the press.

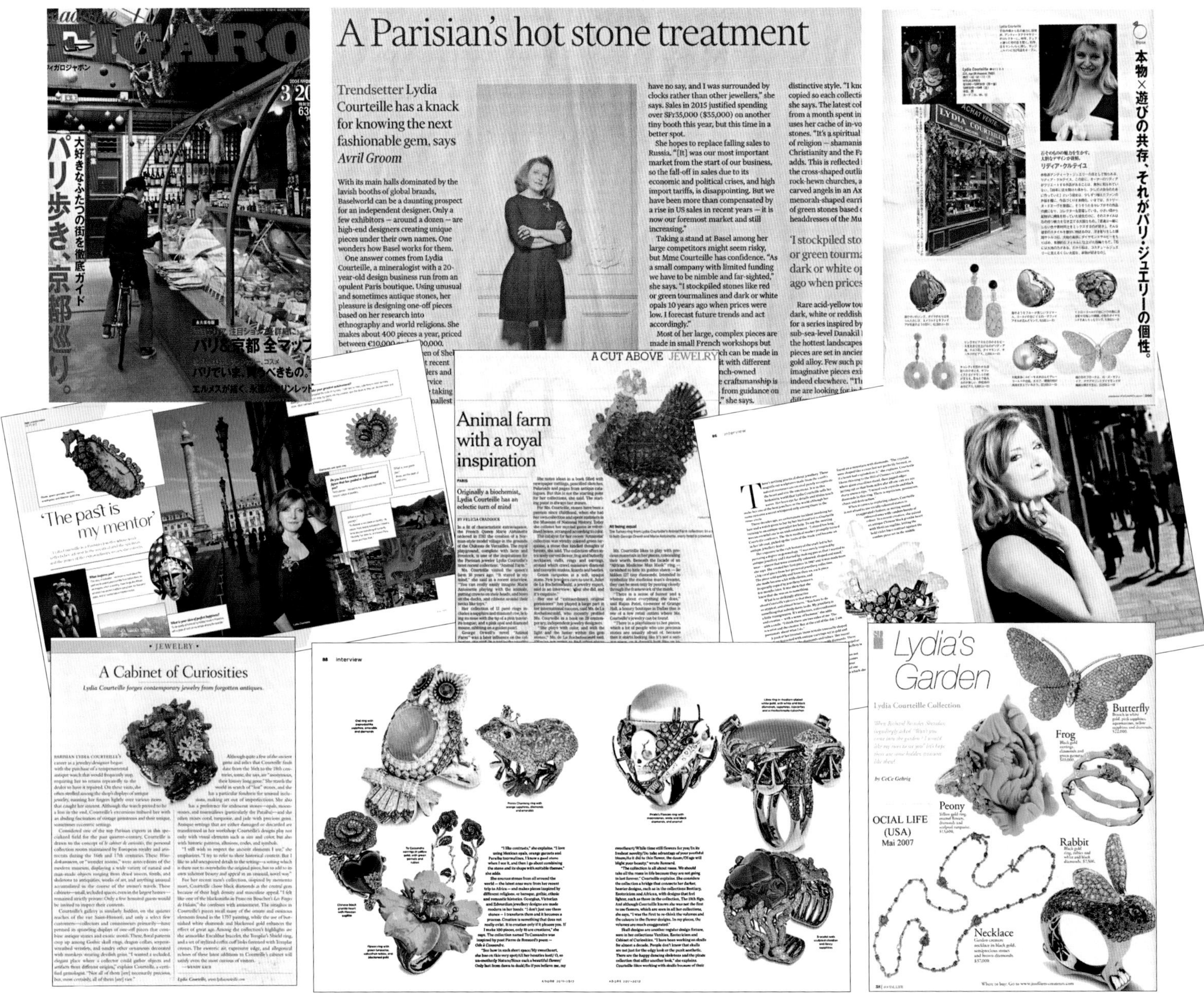

A Parisian's hot stone treatment

Trendsetter Lydia Courteille has a knack for knowing the next fashionable gem, says *Avril Groom*

With its main halls dominated by the lavish booths of global brands, Baselworld can be a daunting prospect for an independent designer. Only a few exhibitors – around a dozen – are high-end designers creating unique pieces under their own names. One wonders how Basel works for them.

One answer comes from Lydia Courteille, a mineralogist with a 20-year-old design business run from an opulent Paris boutique. Using unusual and sometimes antique stones, her pleasure is designing one-off pieces based on her research into ethnography and world religions. She makes about 400 pieces a year, priced between €10,000 [...]

[...] have no say, and I was surrounded by clocks rather than other jewellers," she says. Sales in 2015 justified spending over SFr35,000 ($35,000) on another tiny booth this year, but this time in a better spot.

She hopes to replace falling sales to Russia. "[It] was our most important market from the start of our business, so the fall-off in sales due to its economic and political crises, and high import tariffs, is disappointing. But we have been more than compensated by a rise in US sales in recent years – it is now our foremost market and still increasing."

Taking a stand at Basel among her large competitors might seem risky, but Mme Courteille has confidence. "As a small company with limited funding we have to be nimble and far-sighted," she says. "I stockpiled stones like red or green tourmalines and dark or white opals 10 years ago when prices were low. I forecast future trends and act accordingly."

Most of her large, complex pieces are made in small French workshops but [...]

A CUT ABOVE JEWELRY

Animal farm with a royal inspiration

Originally a biochemist, Lydia Courteille has an eclectic turn of mind

'The past is my mentor'

• JEWELRY •

A Cabinet of Curiosities

Lydia Courteille forges contemporary jewelry from forgotten antiques.

Lydia's Garden

Lydia Courteille Collection

Butterfly

Frog

Peony

Rabbit

Necklace

OCIAL LIFE (USA) Mai 2007

本物×遊びの共存、それがパリ・ジュエリーの個性。

THE INFLUENCE OF LYDIA COURTEILLE'S ANTIQUE JEWELLERY COLLECTION

It is important to look at the jewels that Lydia Courteille collected and sold at the beginning of her career as an antique dealer. They were to have a special influence on her first jewellery designs and in many cases they helped to form an awareness of what was possible to create. They also helped to shape Courteille's taste – she knew what she wanted and what she didn't want to see in her own jewellery designs.

OPPOSITE PAGE:
PORTRAIT OF ÉLISABETH AMÉLIE EUGÉNIE OF WITTELSBACH, DUCHESS OF BAVARIA, EMPRESS OF AUSTRIA BY FRANZ XAVER WINTHALTER, 1865

BELOW:
EARLY 19TH-CENTURY HAIRCOMB, SET *EN TREMBLANT*; DIAMOND, SILVER AND GOLD

"The jewel is a decoration for women, par excellence. ...The art of the jeweller is the recognition of his personality as it so naturally exists in the jewel, to the extent that the memory of those women who wear the jewels is remembered but the artisans who laboured over the piece have long been forgotten and it is she who becomes the designer and true author." *François Mathey*
Chief Curator, Museum of Decorative Arts, Paris, 1967-1985

THIS PAGE:
THREE EARLY 19TH-CENTURY PARURES THAT HAVE PASSED THROUGH LYDIA COURTEILLE'S HANDS

OPPOSITE PAGE:
A 19TH-CENTURY AGATE CAMEO PARURE – AGATE, SEED PEARL, YELLOW GOLD

PARURES

Courteille is well known for her expertise in 18th- and 19th-century parures. During the 18th century, sets comprised a brooch, a pair of earrings, a necklace, a ring, and occasionally shoulder brooches or buckles. In the 19th century, following Napoleon's lead, parures became even more magnificent and sophisticated: they could consist of a pair of bracelets, a brooch, a pair of chandelier or cluster stud earrings, a comb, rings, a necklace, pins and even a belt clasp, as well as a bandeau, diadem or tiara. Much depended on the dress codes and social expectations of the time as to whether the parures were more or less elaborate. Under Napoleon, a keen collector of engraved gemstones, the craze for cameos meant that many were included in parures and were worn by ladies of fashion and influence.

Cameos hold a fascination for Courteille as we shall see in her own collections, and this fascination started through her interest in these forgotten sets of jewellery.

ABOVE:
'SCARLET EMPRESS' CHOKER, c.2014 – RUBELLITE DROPS, DIAMOND, RED RHODIUM-PLATED GOLD
This is an example of how antique jewellery has influenced Courteille's creations.

The diamond star brooches of the Empress Elisabeth of Austria and Queen of Hungary (née Elisabeth de Wittelsbach; 1837-1898) aka "Sissi", also inspired Courteille. The unusual manner of wearing a series of 27 star brooches in the hair as seen in Franz Xaver Winterhalter's portrait, inspired Courteille's taste for romance and the unusual.

In Courteille's 'Scarlet Empress' collection the outlines of 18th-century jewellery are very present. The girandole earrings are one such example, another is her choker, which has all the components of an 18th-century necklace but has been shortened to create a choker, with longer swags that fall onto the wearer's shoulder and breast.

LYDIA COURTEILLE – THE COLLECTOR

One of the most important jewellery designers to be collected by Lydia Courteille is Suzanne Belperron.

Suzanne Belperron

Suzanne Belperron's designs have held an hypnotic attraction for Courteille since 1985, when she first started to collect her pieces, even before the great auction of the Duchess of Windsor's jewels held at Sotheby's Geneva in April 1987. Courteille was attracted by the originality of Belperron's work, which though designed in the 1920s with Boivin and then with Bernard Herz in the 1930s is still as contemporary today as it was then. Belperron had a strong character and knew exactly what she wanted, she had the courage and assurance to go against the trends of the day.

Many of Belperron's most interesting pieces have passed through Courteille's hands. She has been the instigator of several important collections, advising her collectors discreetly and seeking out jewels that can only be defined by their style, as Belperron did not sign her pieces, stating as was the fashion before the war, "My style is my signature".

ABOVE:
FLOWER BROOCH BY SUZANNE BELPERRON – CHALCEDONY, CORAL, DIAMOND, WHITE GOLD

LEFT:
DIADEM CUFFS BY SUZANNE BELPERRON, c.1930s – DIAMOND, WHITE AND YELLOW GOLD, PLATINUM

PROVIDENTIAL MEETINGS AND COLLABORATIONS

PROVIDENTIAL MEETINGS

Throughout her career, Courteille has had chance encounters with many people who have gone on to play an important part in her success.

Art Deco expert Jean-Pierre Camard gave Courteille some valuable advice:

"Work on jewellery as if it were a sculpture, too often in the past jewellery has been considered a minor art but if they are treated as sculpture then they are works of art."

It was a lesson that Courteille never forgot.

Jean-Pierre Brun helped introduce Courteille to the workshops with which she has worked; he was also a mentor, teaching her about the technical intricacies of good workmanship. Brun's workshop collaborated with many of the great jewellery names of the 20th century, such as Suzanne Belperron in her final years, Cartier and Marina B. He says of Courteille's work:

> *"In the future, we will look back at Lydia Courteille's work and realise to what extent they are works of art."*

Karl Lagerfeld was another who encouraged her:

"She has a genius for making jewellery. I trust her taste 100%"

Lagerfeld has been a client since the beginning, buying pieces of Suzanne Belperron jewellery from Lydia Courteille in her early days as an antique jewellery dealer and collector, when she bought Belperron's jewellery purely because she admired their design, long before Belperron became fashionable again. Others who have been by her side since the start of her adventure have been Pierre Bergé and Yves Saint Laurent; in fact, Pierre Bergé was one of the first people to push open the door to her boutique.

OPPOSITE PAGE:
19TH-CENTURY FLORAL DIAMOND EARRINGS
Styled by Loic Masé; Photograph by John Paul Pietrus

BELOW:
KARL LAGERFELD AT THE 62ND ROSE BALL IN MONTE CARLO, 2016, WEARING SUZANNE BELPERRON CLIPS.
© VILLARDS/SIPA/Rex/Shutterstock

OPPOSITE PAGE:
'EXTRA-LUCIDE' COLLECTION, COCAINE RING, EXECUTED IN COLLABORATION WITH LORENZ BÄUMER, c.2005 – ROCK CRYSTAL, DIAMOND AND WHITE GOLD

LEFT: 'EXTRA-LUCIDE' COLLECTION, RING EXECUTED IN COLLABORATION WITH LORENZ BÄUMER, c.1998 – SMOKY QUARTZ, DIAMOND, WHITE GOLD

BELOW:
DESIGN FOR COCAINE RING IN COLLABORATION WITH LORENZ BÄUMER, c.2003

COLLABORATIONS

Over the years, Lydia Courteille has collaborated with many talented artists: from her early years with the atelier Antony and with designers Hervé Boudon and afterwards with Christian Obry and then with Armelle Fontaine who remains by her side today. Marusha Gagro (an art specialist who helped conceive Courteille's first website) spotted the Lithuanian digital artist, Natalie Shau; it was the beginning of a collaboration with Lydia Courteille, which still continues, transforming Courteille's collections into digital universes of their own.

Collaboration with Lorenz Bäumer

In 2006 Courteille asked Lorenz Bäumer to design a 'cocaine' ring based on an idea that she had inspired by the Winter Egg and the ice jewels of Fabergé. It was a ring that was to enter her 'Extra Lucide' collection, which in itself was a satirical play on word and meaning.

In fact, one of her first rings was a collaboration with Lorenz Bäumer.

"It was a stone that I loved, it had this sad air but then again it was as if I had set an explosion, similar to that of Chernobyl, with all its black tourmaline needles inside."

“The Musée des Arts Décoratifs has one of the most extensive and fascinating collections of jewellery and I was delighted when they chose one of my jewels to join their permanent collection. The ring comes from my ‘Autodafe’ collection and reminds me of flat tombstones with small marguerites growing around it – a reflection of how we spend our time on this earth before returning to it”

OPPOSITE PAGE:
‘AUTODAFÉ’ RING DECORATED WITH SMALL MARGUERITES, c.2007 – WHITE ENAMEL, CHAMPAGNE-COLOURED AND BLACK DIAMONDS, BLACK RHODIUM-PLATED GOLD
This ring is exhibited in the permanent collection of the Musée des Arts Décoratifs, Paris.

LYDIA COURTEILLE AT THE MUSÉE DES ARTS DÉCORATIFS, PARIS

Evelyne Possemé and Karine Lacquemant of the Musée des Arts Décoratifs, Paris were part of Courteille’s passage into the past, facilitating visits to the museum. Courteille continues to be a regular visitor to other museums in Paris, such as the Musée Guimet and the Musée du quai Branly. It is in these special places that her ideas and inspiration flow.

Fashion designers have used her forward-thinking jewels for their runways from Prada and Givenchy to Alexis Mabille’s haute couture collection in 2007 and Carven in 2011.

RIGHT:
WINDOW DISPLAY FOR THE 'QUEEN OF SHEBA' COLLECTION, c.2016

OPPOSITE PAGE:
MODEL WEARING JEWELLERY FROM THE 'AMAZONIA' COLLECTION, c.2014
Photograph by Marco Latte

COURTEILLE'S MUSE, WRITER AND PRODUCER, NATHALIE RHEIMS WEARING A PENDANT FROM THE 'CRUSADE' COLLECTION

MADONNA WEARING CREOLE EARRINGS FROM THE 'PIRATE' COLLECTION AT THE LAUNCH OF HER SIGNATURE FRAGRANCE 'TRUTH OR DARE BY MADONNA' IN NEW YORK, 2012

THE THEATRE OF COURTEILLE'S WINDOW DISPLAYS

Each year Courteille creates two magical, theatrical, other-worldly window displays in honour of her most important collections, with the help of Hervé Sauvage and Christian Jacquey.

Guillaume Benoît as photographer joins Natalie Shau, Marco Latte, Thibault Rondoni, Dominique Rondoni, Alain Mairot and Cécile Laurent as part of this creative team.

Her colourful works of art come to life through teamwork with her workshops and, where possible, Courteille has encouraged them to use their artisanal know-how to create jewels that are steeped in tradition and which have been transformed into contemporary statements for strong women with attitude in a modern world.

FAMOUS CLIENTS

These jewels have found homes with many French celebrities, from Mylène Farmer to sisters Bettina and Nathalie Rheims (her muse) and Catherine Deneuve. Outside France, helped by Martyn Laurence Bullard, who opened many doors in Hollywood, great jewellery collectors and stars such as Elizabeth Taylor, Madonna, Nicole Kidman, Brad Pitt and Angelina Jolie have been seduced by Courteille's anarchic appetite for the wild, the beautiful and the extraordinary. Others who have followed Courteille's imagination have been Marylin Gautier, a huge fan of her work, Valentino, Natalia Vodianova, Justin Portman, Daphne Guinness, Alber Elbaz, Riccardo Tisci and Stefanie Renoma; all are enthusiasts of an ever-growing club of those in the know...

INSPIRATION

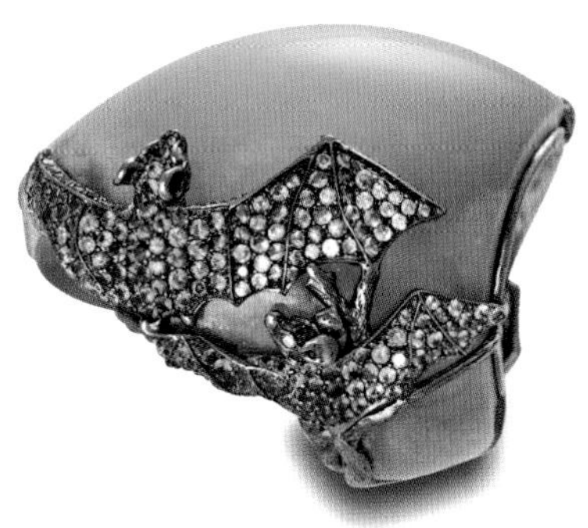

ABOVE:
REAR VIEW OF *ANGE NOIR* (BLACK ANGEL) BY JANINE JANET, c.1980 – BRONZE, QUARTZ CRYSTAL AND TOPAZ CRYSTAL
Courtesy of Thierry Desbenoit et Associés; photograph by Christophe di Pascale

ABOVE LEFT;
'BESTIARY' COLLECTION, BAT RING – CHRYSOPRASE, TSAVORITE GARNETS, DIAMOND, BLACK RHODIUM-PLATED GOLD
Courteille deliberately uses garnets with the diamonds to create a particularly strong contrast between the black gold and the adamantine lustre of the diamonds and the garnet; both stones are singly refractive.

OPPOSITE PAGE:
DETAIL FROM THE CENTRAL PANEL OF THE TRIPTYCH *THE GARDEN OF EARTHLY DELIGHTS* BY HIERONYMUS BOSCH (JHERONIMUS VAN AKEN) 1450-1516
Photograph © Museo Nacional del Prado, Dist. RMN-GP / image du Prado

THE INFLUENCE OF GREAT ARTISTS

Lydia Courteille's jewels start at the source, inspiration comes from all areas of fine art. One such inspiration was the Dutch 15th-century painter, Hieronymus (Jerôme) Bosch. In his paintings, such as *The Seven Deadly Sins and the Four Last Things*, and the triptychs, *The Garden of Earthly Delights*, and *The Temptation of Saint Anthony*, he depicts human bodies and gargoyle style monsters, yet his work was a moralistic view of the Catholic Church's teachings at the time.

> *"You could stand for an hour in front of each detail in this masterpiece, each detail could be a painting in itself."*

How quick they became bats, flying creatures of the night, in Bosch's demonic world, and how quick they were to become friends with the memento mori and to Courteille's dreamlike world.

Texture and colour found in Van Gogh's paintings followed, as did the wonderful gold, often erotic paintings of the Symbolist and Viennese Secessionist painter Gustav Klimt (1862-1918). Then there are the surrealists – Salvador Dalí, Max Ernst and Magritte – who have each influenced Courteille's collections. The complex and busy paintings of Francis Picabia and those of the 19th century Belgian painter Félicien Rops and in particular his illustrations for Charles Baudelaire's book entitled *Les Épaves* published in 1866, are yet other sources for Courteille's creativity.

The shell and mineral sculptures of Janine Janet and the colours of Christian Bérard's stage settings find a place in Courteille's mix, as do the excavations of Egyptologist Sir John Soane.

ABOVE:
LORGNETTE ATTRIBUTED TO RENÉ LALIQUE AND GIVEN AS A GIFT BY SARAH BERNHARDT TO HER 'DAME DE COMPAGNIE'

Sarah Bernhardt's motto 'Quand Même' has been adopted by Lydia Courteille as her own motto.

OPPOSITE PAGE:
NECKLACE BY CHARLES BOUTET DE MONVEL, c.1900 – RUBY, OPAL, GLASS, PEARL, DIAMOND AND GOLD

Private Collection

Photograph by John A. Faier, 2014. © The Richard H. Driehaus Museum.

A world inspired by a jewel – this art nouveau necklace in the form of a spider's web is decorated with small pearls and inhabited by *plique-à-jour* enamel bats with out-stretched wings set *en tremblant*, as well as moths with iridescent opal bodies and beetles set with baroque pearls.

"Abracadraba. Je crée comme je respire. (Abracadabra. I create as I breathe)."
Madelaine Castaing

ABOVE LEFT:
COCKEREL DIADEM BY RENÉ LALIQUE, c.1897 – HORN, AMETHYST, 'PLIQUE-À-JOUR' ENAMEL AND GOLD
©Fondation Calouste Gulbenian, Lisbonne Musée Calouste Gulbenkian; photograph by Carlos Azevedo

ABOVE RIGHT:
COURTEILLE'S 'ANIMAL FARM' COLLECTION, WHICH IS DIRECTLY ASSOCIATED WITH MARIE ANTOINETTE'S HAMLET AT VERSAILLES, INCLUDES THIS SUPERB COCKEREL RING, WHICH IS ALSO INSPIRED BY RENÉ LALIQUE'S FAMOUS COCKEREL HAIR COMB.

CULTURAL INFLUENCES

Madelaine Castaing's adage "Je fais des maisons comme d'autres des poèmes" (I decorate houses as others write poetry) is close to Courteille's heart as she herself creates her jewels. Courteille does in fact start each day by reading a poem; Paul Éluard's the anti-war poem *Liberté* (Liberty; 1942) and the song *Le Déserteur* (The Deserter, 1954) by Boris Vian have both left a lasting impression on her. The great surrealist game 'Cadavre Exquis' (Exquisite corpse) played by such luminaries as André Breton, Marcel Duchamel and Paul Eluard was another key.

Paul Éluard the great poet of the Surrealist movement, and in particular his works *Capitale de la Douleur* (Capital of Paris; 1926) and *L'Amour la Poésie* (Love Poetry; 1929), influenced as much as those by Victor Hugo and the poetry of Ronsard. Courteille was deeply moved by Victor Hugo's poem, which speaks of his life long struggle for the dignity of his fellow man:

La lutte

Ceux qui vivent, ce sont ceux qui luttent; ce sont
Ceux dont un dessein ferme emplit l'âme et le front.
Ceux qui d'un haut destin gravissent l'âpre cime
Ceux qui marchent pensifs, épris d'un but sublime.
Ayant devant les yeux sans cesse, nuit et jour,
Ou quelque saint labeur ou quelque grand amour.
C'est le prophète saint prosterné devant l'arche,
C'est le travailleur, pâtre, ouvrier, patriarche.
Ceux dont le cœur est bon, ceux dont les jours sont pleins.
Ceux-là vivent, Seigneur! les autres, je les plains.
Car de son vague ennui le néant les enivre,
Car le plus lourd fardeau, c'est d'exister sans vivre.

Those who live are those who battle on,
ever holding a clear purpose in mind and spirit,
their lofty destiny scales the jagged peak.
They march forth pondering, enraptured with sublime purpose
The eye ever fixed, day and night,
On some holy task or some great love.
The holy prophet prostrate before the ark,
The labourer, shepherd, workman, patriarch.
The good-hearted, the fulfilled.
The living, Lord! I grieve for all the others.
For they grow drunk on the void of their boredom,
For the heaviest burden is existing without living.*

***CADAVRE EXQUIS* BY MAN RAY, MAX MORISE, ANDRÉ BRETON AND YVES TANGUY, 1928**

Cadavre Exquis – similar in format to the old parlour game 'Consequences', this was developed in the 1920s by André Breton and Pierre Reverdy. It requires each participant to write a sequence, then fold the paper over to conceal it before passing the paper on to the next player to continue the process following a simple rule of writing an 'adjective, noun, adverb, verb'. The resulting phrase is usually comical and nonsensical. The first phrase recorded gave the game its title: 'Le cadavre-exquis-boira-le vin-nouveau' ('The exquisite corpse will drink new wine'). The game can also be played with pictures rather than words. The Surrealists used the game to explore new collaborative methods in writing, film and art.

Photograph courtesy of Sotheby's Inc., © 2011

Films and books – gothic, science fiction and even peplum films – all feed into Courteille's creativity. In particular, the textiles and settings of films such as *Dangerous Liaisons; The Forbidden City* and *The Last Emperor* and more recently the BBC's historical drama series *The Tudors,* have all enriched Courteille's world.

Swashbuckling historical adventures, such as *The Three Musketeers* by Alexandre Dumas, and his home, the Château de Monte-Cristo in Port-Marly to the west of Paris are all part of this rich fabric and along the way, the 'Hall of Mirrors' at Versailles and the small farming hamlet imagined for Marie Antoinette, have all given Courteille flashes of a world that she wanted to bring to life.

* Translation by Yolanda Broad

BELOW LEFT:
'VANITAS' RING, A HAND HOLDING A SKULL IN THE CRUX OF ITS PALM DECORATED ON THE SIDES WITH BONES TAKING UP THE FORM OF A LATIN CROSS – CHAMPAGNE-COLOURED DIAMOND, WHITE DIAMOND, BLACK RHODIUM-PLATED GOLD, WHITE GOLD

BELOW RIGHT:
SALUTING MEMENTO MORI BROOCH – BOULDER OPAL, DIAMOND, WHITE GOLD

SYMBOLS OF REFLECTION

Symbols of reflection and humility are dotted everywhere in Courteille's collections. References to the fashion for 'Vanitas' during the 16th and 17th centuries in Flanders, indicating the brevity of life through butterflies, hourglasses, candles, musical instruments and fading flowers, have all been adopted. Skulls also abound; they hold a fascination for Courteille, as they are all that is left after death has passed by.

“A skeleton is the ultimate proof that you existed and that you lived on Earth.”

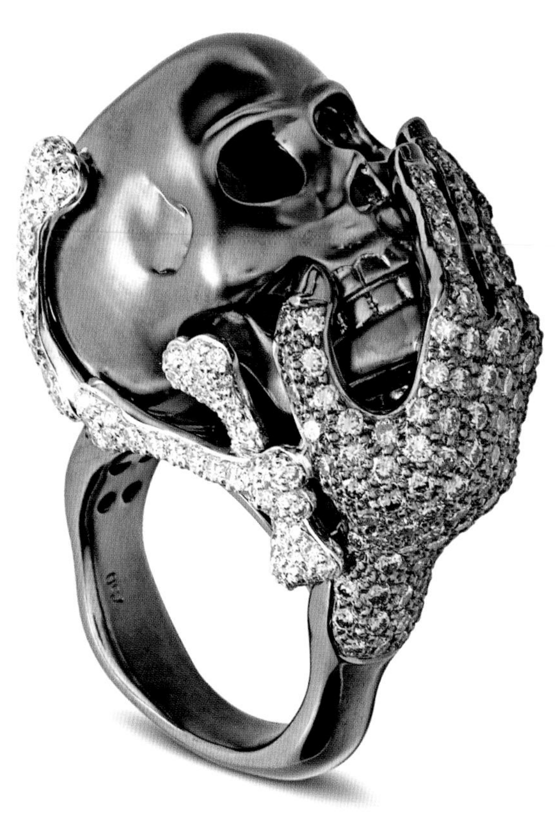

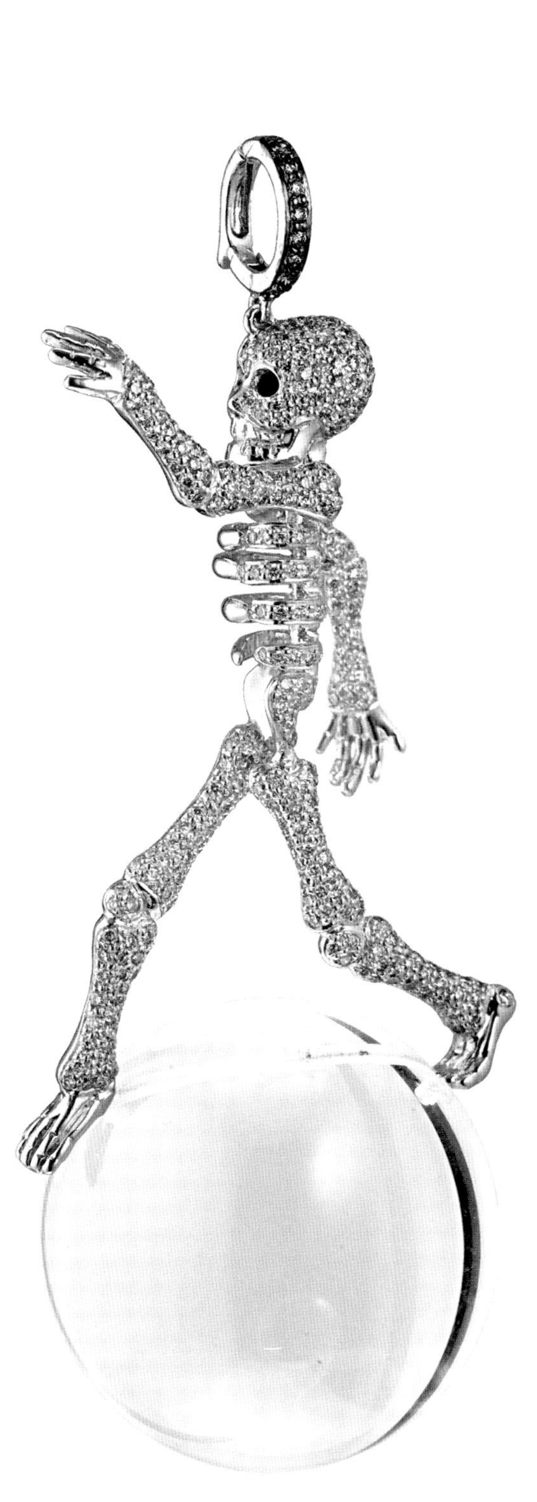

ABOVE:
'VANITAS' RING, CROWNED SKULL, c.2005 – CORAL, DIAMOND, WHITE GOLD

LEFT:
'CATACOMB' COLLECTION, PENDANT, MEMENTO MORI STRIDING ACROSS A ROCK CRYSTAL BOULE – QUARTZ, DIAMOND, WHITE GOLD

STRONG WOMEN

The lives of strong women from history such as Catherine II and Elizabeth I are particularly intriguing. She remembers a visit to the Kremlin in 2007 and being in awe of its splendour. Those who influenced the 20th century, such as Coco Chanel, Madelaine Castaing and Frida Kahlo have all left their imprint on Courteille as well.

> *“I love Frida Kahlo!”*

A Daughter of the '70s

Liliane Schoonjans – aka Lydia Courteille – is a true daughter of the '70s. As an adolescent, she read books by such authors as François Mauriac, she listened to the music of Bob Dylan, Leonard Cohen and Graeme Allwright, a New Zealander by birth who was one of the first to introduce American folk and the protest song to France.

> *“The '70s was a time of freedom, Simone Veil had helped liberate the woman in France. It was a time of hotpants, thigh high boots and a hippie lifestyle. Suddenly everything was possible.”*

Whatever or wherever the source, a provocative Courteille loved to push the boundaries in jewellery design. And yet her open approach is methodical and systematic. She painstakingly researches the basis for each of her collections – collections which depend as much on seeking out the rare and most beautiful gemstones, as they do on her swashbuckling, 'take no prisoners' style.

TOP LEFT: FRIDA KAHLO (1907-1954)

TOP CENTRE: COCO CHANEL
© Sipa Press/REX/Shutterstock

TOP RIGHT: SIMONE VEIL
© Roger Viollet 1975/REX/Shutterstock

ABOVE: STATUE OF JOAN OF ARC AT THE NOTRE-DAME DE ROUEN CATHEDRAL
© Godong/UIG/REX/Shutterstock

OPPOSITE PAGE:
LILIANE SCHOONJANS – HIPPIE STYLE, c.1968

TRAVELS

Courteille's admiration for the great orientalist and adventurer Alexandra David-Néel was a particular catalyst for her travels to faraway places and the impetus for discovering different cultures for herself, bringing back with her the emotions she experienced, to include them into her jewellery for others to see and to sense.

Travels to such places as the Philippines, to Ifugao in the centre of Luzon Island, is another starting point, as it was for her 'Catacombs' collection. Courteille was fascinated by the burial methods of the people who lived there they hollowed out tree trunks into which they placed their dead loved ones and then stacked them one on top of the other in caves within the rock cliffs; with time the wood decays exposing bones from the dead. In other areas, such as Sagada, the hollowed out trunks are suspended on the rock face (probably to protect them from the monsoon floods).

For Courteille, an unusual gemstone that recalls the country in which it is found and its civilisations, is a journey of discovery in itself. It is a reason to start a journey of discovery, of learning; Courteille calls it her *'Effet Pavlovian'* (Pavlovian response).

It was on a journey to Guanajuato in Mexico that she discovered the cult of the Santa Muerte and the intriguing skeleton sweets sold in the streets; it led to her use of Mexican fire opal and to discover another way to contemplate death. Here was a culture that had resisted Christianisation during the period of the Conquistadors and that had kept many of the animist traditions, which continue to live on, alongside those of Christianity.

Another important journey for Courteille, was her discovery of the subterranean cities of Cappadocia in Turkey such as Derinkuyu and Kaymaklı. These large multi-level underground cities were probably first built by the Phrygians during the 8th-7th centuries BC. They were later expanded by Christians living there to escape persecution.

ABOVE LEFT:
MANY OF THE OLDER TATTOOED WOMEN IN THE BONTOC TRIBE ON THE ISLAND OF LUZON WEAR SERPENT SKELETONS AS HAIRPIECES FOR GOOD LUCK

ABOVE RIGHT:
DECAYING TREE TRUNK SARCOPHAGUS ON THE ISLAND OF LUZON

OPPOSITE PAGE:
'VANITAS' RING, c.2007 – NETSUKE SKULL SURROUNDED BY SEVEN ANCIENT EGYPTIAN SCARABS, TSAVORITE GARNET, RUBY, BLACK DIAMOND, RED ENAMEL, BLACK RHODIUM-PLATED GOLD
Photograph by Thibaut Rondoni

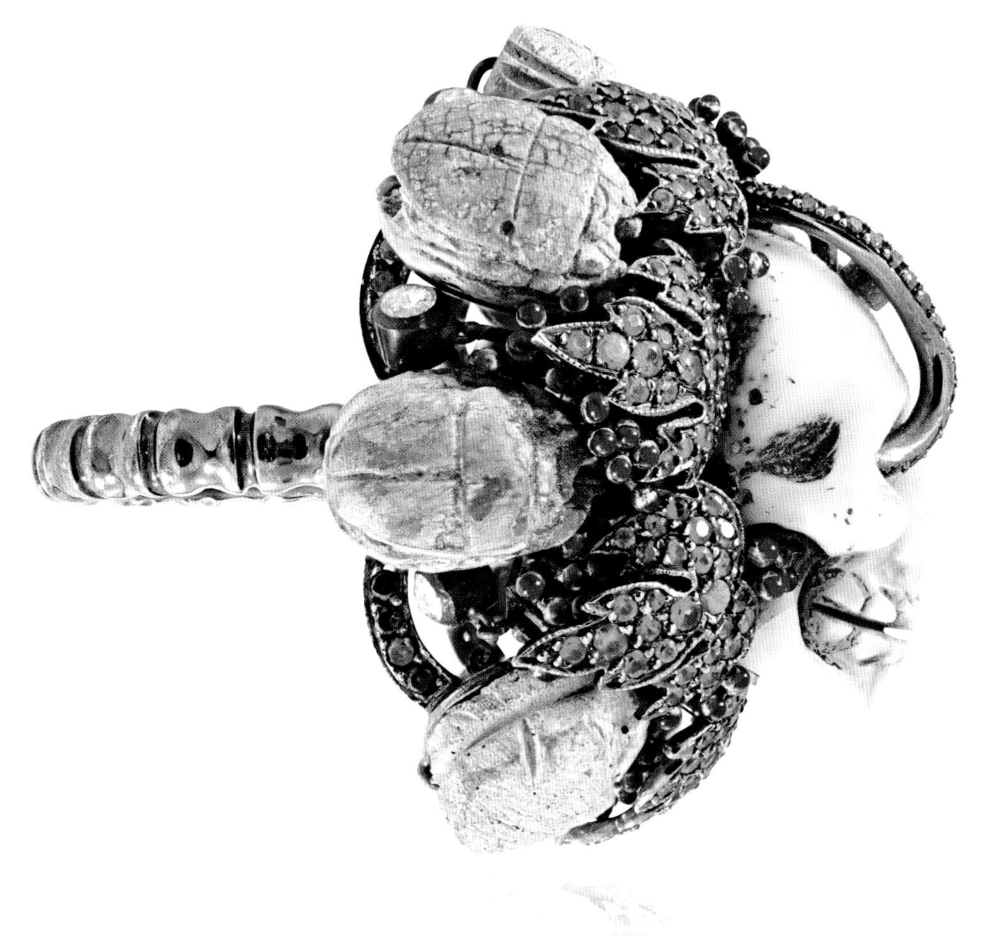

TRAVEL THROUGH GEMSTONES

The random process by which gemstones seem to be formed in certain parts of the world has always intrigued Courteille; that just the correct quantity of chromium or iron, for instance, has been mixed with other chemical substances; that they should come together to form a gemstone of intense colour and lustre, so many millions of years ago, is extraordinary. It touches the very essence of what Jacques Monod wrote in *Chance and Necessity*, the complete mystery of its randomness.

> *"Through my jewels, I want people to discover the natural treasures that exist and their beauty; people ignore the journeys through time that each of these gemstones have made on this planet."*

Courteille's interest has been such that she has visited many of the mines from which her gemstones have originated. The Larimar mines near Santo Domingo and the opal mines at Magdalena in the Jalisco region of Mexico hold no secret. The gold mines of Minas Gerais and those in Sri Lanka where moonstone is mined were others to be visited. The idea is not only to discover where the gemstones have by chance been created but also to meet the people, the miners who have helped to initiate the chain of events that will produce her jewels. Her conversations and all that she learns from these miners are used as a catalyst for what she will eventually do with the gemstones that she acquires. Curiosity has also led to a trip to La Paz, Baja California in Mexico to discover their special natural pearls and also to exchanges with the fishermen in Pedernales, on the border between the Dominican Republic and Haiti, who dive for the pink pearls she uses in her work.

ABOVE:
'EARLY' RING – LARIMAR, MULTI-COLOURED GARNETS, WHITE GOLD

RIGHT:
LYDIA COURTEILLE VISITING THE LARIMAR MINE IN SANTO DOMINGO

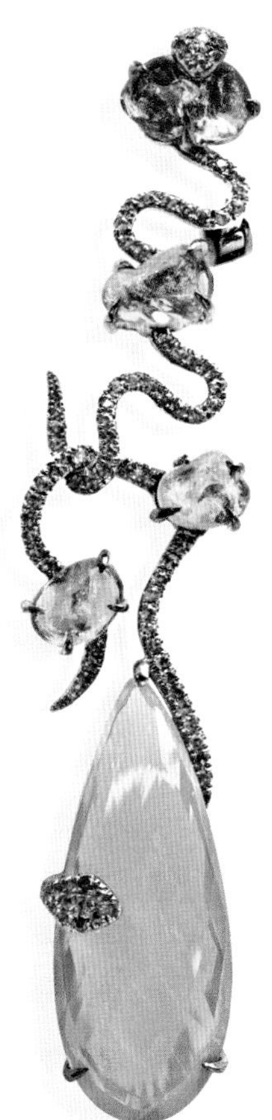

“A journey of discovery to the countries of gemstones and their civilisations.”

ABOVE LEFT:
'XOCHIMILCO' COLLECTION, LIZARD RING, c.2010 – MEXICAN FIRE OPAL, TSAVORITE GARNET, RUBY, BLACK RHODIUM-PLATED GOLD

ABOVE RIGHT:
'XOCHIMILCO' COLLECTION, SERPENT PENDANT EARRINGS – MEXICAN FIRE OPAL, TSAVORITE GARNET, RUBY, BLACK RHODIUM-PLATED GOLD

LEFT:
'BESTIARY' COLLECTION RING DEPICTING BATS, c.2004 – ROCK CRYSTAL INCLUDED WITH MOSS AGATE, RUBY, CHAMPAGNE-COLOURED DIAMOND, BLACK RHODIUM-PLATED GOLD
After a design by Hervé Boudon.

'CATACOMB' VANITAS PENDANT, c.2005 – TIGER CLAWS, CHAMPAGNE-COLOURED DIAMOND, WHITE DIAMOND, BLACK RHODIUM-PLATED GOLD

On a trip to Namibia, Courteille thought that she would find some magnificent tourmalines. Alas she found none, and she had to content herself with a series of unusual and inspired finds. A quartz crystal was one that she transformed into a ring for the 'Autodafé' collection. In another shop she also found some tiger claws, which she made into a pendant and led to the 'Or Fetiche' collection. Other pieces led to the 'Catacomb' collection.

THE CREATIVE PROCESS

Courteille's creative process starts with the gemstone, the gemstones that 'speak' to her. They may spend a month, a year or even ten sitting in her safe waiting to be used. From this point, inspiration comes slowly, it might be triggered by the background colour in a fresco and the marriage of that colour with the nuances within the gemstone.

A journey taken years before may be the catalyst and from this point Courteille will chose her theme and then bring in other ideas from history and literature, which can bring a duality and a story to the jewel. She puts her ideas on paper, making a quick drawing, and communicates her wishes to one of the many workshops with which she collaborates. Wax models are created and the discussion continues until Courteille is satisfied with the size and the proportions of the piece.

THE GEOLOGIST

Lydia Courteille plays with the gift of light and brightness within a gemstone as well as using the surface lustres to contrast and complement each other, as she creates.

She is known for the unusual and extraordinary quality of the gemstones that she uses; she is always on the lookout for new gemstones, glyptics and cameos with a strong cultural connection. She describes herself as a frustrated geologist/archaeologist looking for a balance in her life where she can be both a scientist and a creator. She lives in a symbiotic relationship with her gemstones, they are her silent partners.

From the huge deep glowing red rubellites in the 'Scarlet Empress' collection to the heavily included rock crystal gemstones, she seeks out those stones that have a story to tell, such as her Cocaine ring from the 'Extra Lucide' collection.

ABOVE LEFT:
'EXTRA-LUCIDE' VANITAS RING, c.2006 – QUARTZ, DIAMOND, WHITE GOLD

ABOVE RIGHT:
'SCARLET EMPRESS' ASYMMETRIC EARRINGS, c.2013 – RUBY, RUBELLITE DROPS, RED RHODIUM-PLATED GOLD

BELOW, LEFT:
CAMEO & GLYPTIC *HABILLAGE* RING, PORTRAIT OF A LADY, c.2012 – SARDONYX, TRANSLUCENT RED HOT ENAMEL, DIAMOND, SILVER, WHITE GOLD, YELLOW GOLD

BELOW, RIGHT:
'STAR DUST' GALAXY RING, c.2008 – DRUSY CRYSTAL, RUBY, BLACK AND WHITE DIAMOND, BLACK RHODIUM-PLATED GOLD

CARVINGS AND COURTEILLE'S 'HABILLAGE' JEWELS

Carved gems, either modern or ancient, have also found their way into Courteille's collections. The magnificent early 20th-century portrait sculptures from her 'Or Fetiche' collection were sourced from flea markets and auctions.

As well as tribal masks and their use in tribal rituals and symbolism in Africa, Courteille produced a colourful and highly original collection, which compares to none. Ivory and wooden carvings were gathered for size, beauty and sculptural qualities as well as for their imagery.

FAR LEFT:
'CAMEO & GLYPTIC' *HABILLAGE* RING, 19TH-CENTURY 'PORTRAIT OF A BLACKAMOOR', c.2006 – 19TH-CENTURY SARDONYX CAMEO, TRANSLUCENT GREEN ENAMEL, RUBY, DIAMOND, SILVER, YELLOW GOLD

LEFT:
'BESTIARY' COLLECTION, SERPENT AND SALAMANDER RING – AZURITE CRYSTAL, TSAVORITE GARNET, CHAMPAGNE-COLOURED DIAMOND, BLACK RHODIUM-PLATED GOLD

BELOW LEFT:
'OR FETICHE' COLLECTION, *HABILLAGE* BRACELET, c.2008 – ANTIQUE IVORY SCULPTURE, DIAMOND, YELLOW GOLD

BELOW RIGHT:
'OR FETICHE' COLLECTION, *HABILLAGE* BROOCH, c.2008 – ANTIQUE IVORY SCULPTURE, DIAMOND, YELLOW GOLD

ABOVE LEFT:
'SECRET GARDEN' COLLECTION, SCULPTED ORCHID RING, c.2008 – SUGELITE, SAPPHIRE, DIAMOND, BLACK RHODIUM-PLATED GOLD, WHITE GOLD

ABOVE RIGHT:
'SECRET GARDEN' COLLECTION, SCULPTED ORCHID BROOCH, c.2004 – CARVED WATERMELON TOURMALINE, TSAVORITE GARNET, DIAMOND, BLACK RHODIUM-PLATED GOLD, WHITE GOLD

She started by adorning them with gold and diamond earrings and hair pieces; they were part of her 'Habillage' jewels. Cameos were given the same treatment and found homes in the 'Cameo and Glyptic' collection.

From these beginnings came her insects, colonising splendidly huge orchid dress rings and brooches in sugilite and watermelon tourmaline, which all spilled over into her 'Cabinet de Curiosité' collection.

Amulets and carved gems from ancient Egypt were transformed into bracelets and 'vanitas'. Japanese ivory netsuke are dressed with serpents, swords, crosses and Egyptian scarabs. Lava, shell, sardonyx, micro-mosaics and Limoges enamel have all been given the Courteille treatment, given a second life, to become modern jewels with stories to tell. Jade in all its colours - black, green, lavender, ochre and white has been transformed into cabbage rings and jade plaques have been possessed by dragons and serpents.

'BESTIARY' COLLECTION, SERPENT AND DRAGON BRACELET, c.2006 – BLUE AMBER, TSAVORITE GARNET, CHAMPAGNE- AND COGNAC-COLOURED DIAMOND, WHITE DIAMOND, BLACK RHODIUM-PLATED GOLD
Blue amber comes from just outside Santo Domingo in the Dominican Republic. It derives its very special colour from volcanic ash. The bracelet represents Courteille's duality by using Eastern and Western representations of the the serpent and the dragon.

ABOVE: 'GYPSET' COLLECTION, ASYMMETRIC EARRINGS, c.2015 – TRANSLUCENT *PLIQUE-À-JOUR* ENAMEL, BLUE AND PINK SAPPHIRE, BLACK RHODIUM-PLATED GOLD, WHITE GOLD

Photograph by Thibaut Rondoni

OPPOSITE PAGE, LEFT:
'BESTIARY' LIZARD RING, c.2006 – AQUAMARINE, TSAVORITE GARNET, DIAMOND, BLACK RHODIUM-PLATED GOLD, WHITE GOLD

OPPOSITE PAGE, RIGHT:
'EXTRA-LUCIDE' COLLECTION, VANITAS RING, c.2014 – QUARTZ, CHAMPAGNE-COLOURED DIAMOND, BLACK RHODIUM-PLATED GOLD

TRADITIONAL AND CUTTING-EDGE TECHNIQUES

She encourages the workshops to excel at what they do best, in many cases using their traditional techniques to give them a new outlook and also to help encourage their transmission to the next generation. These can be seen in the use of enamel work in the 'Gypset' and the 'Vendange Tardive' collections.

In other jewels, Courteille uses the possibilities of new technology to enhance the range of her collections. She uses lasers to create a form of intaglio within the stone to create *memento mori,* which seem to have been there since the formation of the rock crystal.

In her 'Zodiac' collection, Courteille uses titanium, and the versatility of its colours, to enhance sugelite. Most collections include her signature 18-carat black rhodium-plated gold with which she invariably matches black and champagne-coloured diamonds. Depending on her intention, she sets white diamonds in black rhodium-plated gold for contrast, or in white gold if she is looking for a clean, bright finish.

“I used to buy large groups of small gemstones but I very quickly realised that I would be better off buying the important gemstones for the centre of my creations and to leave the workshop to set the smaller gemstones. When I wanted to pavé-set gemstones, I never had the right sizes so I quickly realised that it was better to let the atelier find them. Now I only buy the central gemstones.”

DESIGN AND DUALITY

“Culture. Emotion. Creation.”

Lydia Courteille’s jewellery is inspired by her own brew of duality. It is born *of “a gourmandise, a voraciousness and a bulimia for jewellery*”. Hers is a Manichean point of view: the struggle between good (a spiritual world of light) and evil (a material world of dark). It is also simply about opposites: masks of happiness and sadness, sweet and sour etc. Courteille has always been fascinated with archaeology and geology and her interests come together to create jewels that challenge with their references to culture and to history. Thought-provoking though they are, they also have a humorous, lightly ironic, subversive and rebellious touch, a Courteille hallmark. She is part of the anti-conformist brigade.

The ‘Xochimilco’ collection combines Mexican folk tradition with the beautiful play of colour in Mexican fire opals. The ‘Animal Farm’ collection marries George Orwell’s *Animal Farm* with Marie Antoinette; while the ‘Scarlet Empress’ collection brings together the colour red with Soviet Communism, 18th-century jewellery, and Catherine the Great and the cruelty of a period when a life was worth less than nothing. Von Sternberg’s 1934 film *The Scarlet Empress*, which greatly shocked the Catholic Church because of the lack of morality, is yet another layer to Courteille’s ‘Scarlet Empress’ collection. ‘A Cassandre’ is about the brevity of beauty and youth, symbolised by pink roses, as well as symbolising the doomsayer, who no-one will believe.

Intrigued by the quote often attributed to the essence of Karl Marx’s teachings *“Religion is the opium of the people”,* Courteille has set out to demystify the cultural and religious beliefs of various peoples. Baroque and Gothic references are at play in much of Courteille’s colourful work and her combinations are deliberately atypical, creating a dialogue between the past, the present and the future just as they are a conversation between the designer, the wearer and the admirer.

ABOVE:
‘SCARLET EMPRESS’ COLLECTION, HAREM RING – RED TOURMALINE, RUBY, RED RHODIUM-PLATED GOLD
Note the juxtaposition of the Soviet hammer-and-sickle symbol with those of the double-headed eagle and the entwined ‘C’ for Catherine the Great, also the colour red representing both communism and the cruelty of Catherine the Great’s reign.

OPPOSITE PAGE:
LYDIA COURTEILLE IN THE PLACE VENDOME

“I always try and present both the exotic and dark aspects of humanity and nature. Jewellery is supposed to show the sweet, glamorous side of life, but my pieces are between fine jewellery and art. It’s crucial that they show the dark and subversive side of the modern times in which we live; the century is violent, and I show that in my work.”

ABOVE LEFT:
‘A CASSANDRE’ COLLECTION, RING – AMETHYST, TSAVORITE GARNET, BLACK DIAMOND, BLACK RHODIUM-PLATED GOLD

ABOVE RIGHT:
‘SECRET GARDEN’ COLLECTION, SCULPTED BLACK ONYX ROSE RING – ONYX, RUBY, TSAVORITE GARNET, CHAMPAGNE-COLOURED DIAMOND, YELLOW GOLD

OPPOSITE PAGE:
MONKEY BRACELET – ANGEL SKIN CORAL, RUBY, GREEN GARNET, BLACK DIAMOND,BLACK RHODIUM-PLATED GOLD
The monkey and the rose are associated with longevity in Chinese art and in the Western world the rose is often used as a symbol of beauty and youth.

ABOVE:
'ABYSSE' COLLECTION, FLYING FISH RING, c.2008 – BOULDER OPAL, PURPLE AND BLUE SAPPHIRE, TSAVORITE GARNET, DIAMOND, BLACK RHODIUM-PLATED GOLD

RIGHT:
'BESTIARY' COLLECTION, TWO-HEADED SERPENT RING, c.2007 – GARNET, PERIDOT, BLACK RHODIUM-PLATED GOLD

BELOW:
'AMAZONIA' COLLECTION, FLOWER RING, c.2011 – GREEN TURQUOISE, CABOCHON RUBY, BLACK RHODIUM-PLATED GOLD

ABOVE:
'XOCHIMILCO' COLLECTION, SUN BRACELET – FIRE OPAL, ORANGE SAPPHIRE, RUBY, SPESSARTITE GARNET, TEXTURED BLACK RHODIUM-PLATED GOLD

As a child, Courteille had both a scientific and a creative mind, a dual personality that she nurtured through hours of sketching and imagining; she could see in her mind's eye, concoctions in sequins and embroidery flamboyantly strutting down the cat-walk, whilst also diligently studying the parts of insects through a microscope (a present from her father), as if she were a true entomologist.

As an adult, she looked for a way to bring all her interests together in a way that would earn her a good living as well as doing something that she loved. Lydia Courteille Creations became her *Maslow pyramid*, which she is still building. Her approach to her designs is that of a scientist and an ethnologist. She delves into a subject the same way in which an explorer might study a new continent, to discover and to demystify; she investigates, she researches and she experiments, until she has found what she is looking for:

" Principle, procedure, conclusion, as in chemistry"

An epicurean at heart, she loves the search, the challenge of finding beautiful objects and then transforming them into a jewel that has not yet been created – a jewel that must enhance the beauty and interest of the wearer; it must converse. There is poetry, an invitation to dream and to enter another world in each of her jewels – they are *'Conversation Jewels'*.

IDEAS BEHIND THE COLLECTIONS

"It was a bright cold day in April, and the clocks were striking thirteen."

1984 by George Orwell

The four-leaf clover stretches out over the Parisian footpath beckoning and glistening gold in the afternoon sun. The small jewellery shop is snugly located, close to the famous Place Vendôme and the Tuileries. The windows of this little boutique are always full of fascinating jewel sculptures evoking dreams, fairy tales as well as the more provocative themes of the passing of time and the brevity of life. They are jewels that are subversive, humorous and thought provoking, in Courteille's window displays, as in the vitrines inside, they are the actors on the stage performing for the on-lookers as they pass by.

ABOVE:
A PAIR OF EARRINGS FROM THE 'CATACOMB' COLLECTION, c.2009 – BLACK AND WHITE DIAMOND, BLACK RHODIUM-PLATED GOLD, WHITE GOLD
The crossbones/four-leaf clovers at the top demonstrate Courteille's use of duality in meaning.

OPPOSITE PAGE:
INTERIOR OF LYDIA COURTEILLE'S BOUTIQUE, c.2011, SHOWING THE 'XOCHIMILCO' COLLECTION (c.2010), IN THE DISPLAY CASE IN THE FOREGROUND
Photograph by J. Pepion

BELOW:
VANITAS WINDOW DISPLAY SHOWING THE 'VENDANGE TARDIVE' COLLECTION, IN COLLABORATION WITH HERVÉ SAUVAGE, c.2013
Photograph by Guillaume Benoît

The melodious chiming of the boutique bell hints at a past packed with moments and people. On entering the ultramarine jewellery box, the snug warmth of wood wraps itself around the caller. Courteille has swathed in blue, the dark wooden columns and latticework shielding the brightly lit vitrines, which beguile and hypnotise; where does reality stop and the dream begin?

In homage to the window displays by the hugely talented Leïla Menchari for Hermès, Lydia Courteille has called upon the help of such artists as Hervé Sauvage to create theatrical scenes that are both unusual and unique, bringing her passion for scenery to life.

“*I love when the window is full – it represents abundance and opulence.*”

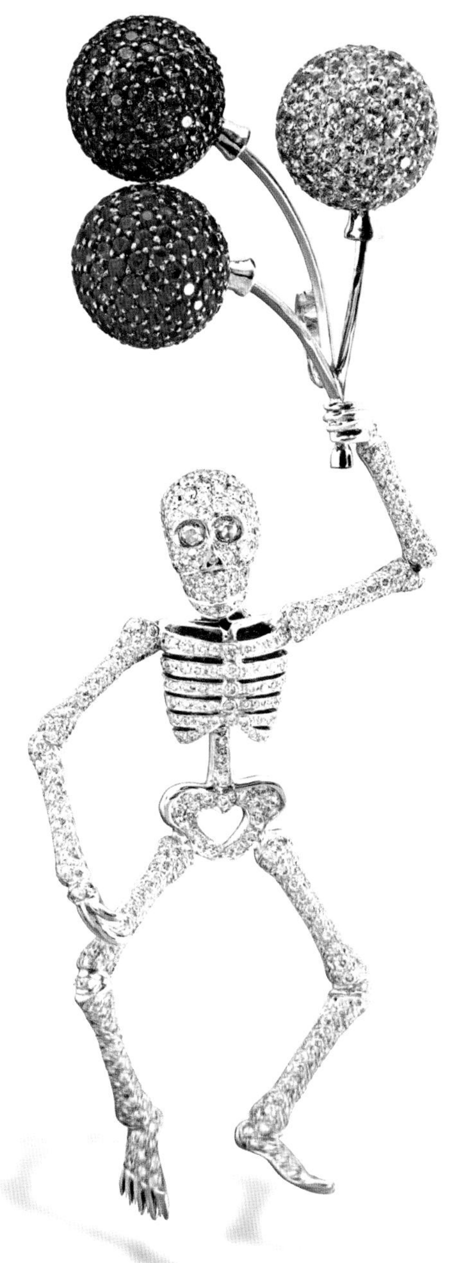

ABOVE LEFT:
'CATACOMB' COLLECTION BROOCH OF A SKELETON HOLDING BALLOONS, c.2010 – RUBY, SAPPHIRE, DIAMOND, WHITE GOLD

ABOVE RIGHT:
'VANITAS' RING FEATURING COURTEILLE'S ICONIC SKULL AND CROSSBONES, c.2005 – CHAMPAGNE-COLOURED DIAMOND, WHITE DIAMOND, BLACK RHODIUM-PLATED GOLD, WHITE GOLD

In the shop window: the vanitas are on display, the hour glass counts the passing of seconds and minutes; a flower that has seen better days, a petal already fallen; the skull stares out, a reminder of death, of life and moments of beauty and happiness, fleeting and transient. There are testimonies of dreams, of memories: a diamond skeleton in white gold is walking by, his arm outstretched holding balloons in vibrant red, yellow and blue, he seems to be offering his joyful bounty to the onlooker.

BELOW RIGHT:
DESIGN FROM THE 'TOPKAPI' COLLECTION FOR A RING DEPICTING A TURBANED MAN LOOKING INTO A CRYSTAL BALL TO SEE WHERE HIS DESTINY MAY LEAD HIM
Gouache by Armelle Fontaine

BOTTOM:
'RAINBOW WARRIOR' RING, THE CHIEF STARES INTO HIS CRYSTAL BALL AND SEES THE FUTURE: THE AMERICAN FLAG – SAPPHIRE, TSAVORITE GARNET, RUBY, QUARTZ, ENAMEL (RED, TURQUOISE, WHITE, YELLOW AND BROWN), BLACK DIAMOND, CHAMPAGNE-COLOURED DIAMOND, YELLOW GOLD

COLLECTIONS

Each year Lydia Courteille creates two to four jewellery collections, the first is cerebral with references to historical, social and politically charged themes accompanied by her unusual and stunning gemstones. The second collection is lighter and less expensive, it works laterally and uses regular themes found individually in her main collections. They help create a unity between each collection and help people to recognise the threads that gather her collections together, creating a richly woven tapestry of DNA that is exclusively hers; her magical 'dreamprint'.

To cite one or two examples, her 'Sweet and Sour' collection in phosphosiderite*, was born from her prize-winning green turquoise 'Amazonia' collection, just as her 'Alizarine' collection was the starting point for her 'Scarlet Empress' collection.

* Phosphosiderite or 'la rosa voca' (pink stone) is a soft gemstone similar in texture to that of jade. It was first discoved in 1890 in South Africa and in Chile it is found in nodules of purple and bright pink scattered in the Atacama region of the Andes mountain range. The stone's lavenders and purples are found in Germany, Portugal and in the United States at the Blue Moose Mine in Custer, South Dakota.

'SECRET GARDEN' COLLECTION, LILY OF THE VALLEY, *HAREM RING* WITH MATCHING ASYMMETRIC EARRINGS – TSAVORITE GARNET, PEARL, DIAMOND, WHITE GOLD, BLACK RHODIUM-PLATED GOLD

USE OF COLOUR

Colour is the key to all of Courteille's jewels, her use of gemstones with strong colours and sense of place are deliberate attempts to trigger a Pavlovian reflex so that the Australian opal blues of her 'Abysse' collection evoke the sea and memories of holidays gone by, whilst the fire and bright oranges of Mexican opal are joyous, bringing to mind the sun and the heat of summer, as well as their association with the history and culture of Mexico. The greens in her 'Amazonia' collection elicit memories of wellbeing, the outdoors and bucolic images of tropical forests. Her mastery of colour in such collections as 'Purple Fiction' and 'Sweet and Sour' is demonstrated here with the use of pink phosphosiderite from South Africa and Chile.

BELOW LEFT:
'SWEET & SOUR' COLLECTION, FLOWER RING, c.2013 – PHOSPHOSIDERITE, YELLOW TOURMALINE, YELLOW SAPPHIRE, YELLOW GOLD

BELOW RIGHT:
'AMAZONIA' COLLECTION, FLOWER RING, c.2011 – GREEN TURQUOISE, YELLOW TOURMALINE, CHAMPAGNE-COLOURED DIAMOND, TSAVORITE GARNET, EMERALD, YELLOW GOLD

Courteille mixed them with rubies, sapphires and tanzanite for her small collection, 'Purple Fiction' (a play on words, referencing the cult film *Pulp Fiction* by Quentin Tarantino.)

In each case she found that the appearance was subdued and almost classic. She loved the bright candy-floss colour of the phosphosiderites and, undeterred, she worked on the new collection, 'Sweet and Sour'. This time she concentrated on playing with the matt lemon yellow cacoxenite veins and she used bright yellow beryl and yellow sapphire, lemon tourmaline and pale yellow diamond to *"wake up the sleepy yellow veins"*.

Courteille wanted to arouse people's emotions, and with this collection, does just that; she had found the *"perfect marriage"*.

'PURPLE FICTION' ORCHID RING, c.2015 – PHOSPHOSIDERITE, TANZANITE, RUBY, TSAVORITE GARNET, CHAMPAGNE-COLOURED DIAMOND, BLACK RHODIUM-PLATED GOLD, YELLOW GOLD

> *"I found them by chance. Gemstones must evoke something in me; they must speak to me and then I create a collection around them."*

ABOVE LEFT:
'SENS INTERDIT' COLLECTION, *CROQUESE DE DIAMANT* (FORTUNE HUNTER) RING, c.2009 – RUBY, QUARTZ, DIAMOND, BLACK RHODIUM-PLATED GOLD, WHITE GOLD

ABOVE RIGHT:
'SENS INTERDIT' COLLECTION, *MANGEUR DE GRENOUILLES* (DEVOURER OF FROGS) RING, c.2010 – RUBY, TSAVORITE GARNET, DIAMOND, BLACK RHODIUM-PLATED GOLD

OPPOSITE PAGE:
'SWEET & SOUR' COLLECTION, ORCHID RING, c.2013 – PHOSPHOSIDERITE, YELLOW TOURMALINE, YELLOW SAPPHIRE, DIAMOND, YELLOW GOLD

UNPREDICTABILITY

This ability to incite emotion and a reaction to her jewels – be it decadent, sensual or ironic – is a freedom that only the independent jewellery designer has. At any one time, Courteille may be designing a jewel that is as much about glamour as it is a work of contemporary art and then suddenly she will do something quite unpredictable, bringing out the 'bad girl', provocative side in her design style. An interesting example is her 'Croquese de Diamant' ring (Fortune Hunter) from the 'Sens Interdit' collection (No Entry), which is suddenly transformed in a total break from before, into a 'Mangeur de Grenouilles' (Devourer of frogs), which becomes an interesting parody on French/British relations, or could it be a little surprise from the chef? Courteille's inspiration for this collection comes from the sensual if provocative film *Nine and a Half Weeks,* directed by Adrian Lyne and starring Kim Basinger in 1986.

"I love symbols and I think that glamour should be part of a jewel and reside in the themes that it explores; so I imagine the shape of lips which eat a strawberry, explore the marriage of women with flowers. I am trying to bring a different interpretation to these eternal themes. Flowers underline a woman's femininity but I also like to break that comfortable image by adding insects."

EARLY PIECES

ABOVE LEFT:
'SECRET GARDEN' COLLECTION, FLORAL RING – RED CORAL, DIAMOND, BLACK ENAMEL, GOLD
This was one of Lydia Courteille's very first rings.

ABOVE CENTRE:
VANITAS RING, c.2002 – OPAL, BLACK RHODIUM-PLATED WHITE GOLD

ABOVE RIGHT:
CITRUS RING, c.2002 – AMETHYST, YELLOW AND WHITE DIAMOND, ENAMEL, YELLOW GOLD
Lydia Courteille can be seen wearing this ring in her portrait opposite

LEFT:
CONE BRACELET, c.2002 – TURQUOISE, LAPIS LAZULI, YELLOW GOLD

OPPOSITE PAGE:
PORTRAIT OF LYDIA COURTEILLE, c.2004, WEARING A 'FILLES DU CIEL' CORAL PLAQUE RING AND AN EARLY AMETHYST RING DECORATED WITH ENAMEL LEAVES AND SMALL CITRUS FRUIT (SEE THIS PAGE, TOP RIGHT)

OPPOSITE PAGE:
'RAINING STARS' EARRINGS, c.2003 – DIAMOND, WHITE GOLD

ABOVE LEFT:
FROG RING, c.2005 – AMETHYST, TSAVORITE GARNET, PINK AND BLUE SAPPHIRE, RUBY, BLACK RHODIUM-PLATED GOLD, YELLOW GOLD
Design By Hervé Boudon.

ABOVE RIGHT:
'MADAME BUTTERFLY' RING – AMETHYST, TSAVORITE GARNET, DIAMOND, BLACK RHODIUM-PLATED GOLD

RIGHT:
'SUNSET' RING – ROCK CRYSTAL, MOONSTONE, DIAMOND, YELLOW GOLD

THE NEW DECOR FOR LYDIA COURTEILLE'S BOUTIQUE, 2011
Photograph by J.Pepion

THE COLLECTIONS

FILLES DU CIEL

PREVIOUS SPREAD:
JEWELS ON DISPLAY AT THE MOSCOW WORLD FINE ART FAIR IN 2006
LYDIA COURTEILLE'S CARVED PLAQUE JEWELS IN JADE, CORAL AND TURQUOISE.
CONE BRACELET, c.2002 – LAPIS LAZULI AND TURQUOISE, YELLOW GOLD;
ORCHID BROOCH, c.2004 – AMETHYST, LAVENDER JADE, GREEN GARNET, GOLD;
SPIDER CREOLE EARRINGS, c.2003 – DIAMOND, BLACK ENAMEL, WHITE GOLD

BELOW:
'BESTIARY' GLYPTIC RING – TURQUOISE, RUBY, GREEN GARNET, BLACK RHODIUM-PLATED GOLD

FILLES DU CIEL (1998)

Courteille introduces us straight away to her signature playfulness with 'Filles du Ciel', – Daughters of Heaven – which is a play on 'Fils du Ciel' (Son of Heaven), a title used to describe the Emperor of China.

This was one of Lydia Courteille's first collections. Taking her cue from Asian sculpted jade plaques and an extremely rare turquoise sculpted insect, similar to a netsuke, she decided to carve turquoise and coral in a similar way. This might seem obvious now, but as so often happens with a simple inspired idea, no one had thought to question what had been the norm. Courteille mounted them into rings within garland-style borders.

The novelty was their oversized proportions and her use of what were, at the time, considered unusual colour combinations. Other rings followed, in jade and coral, as well as turquoise.

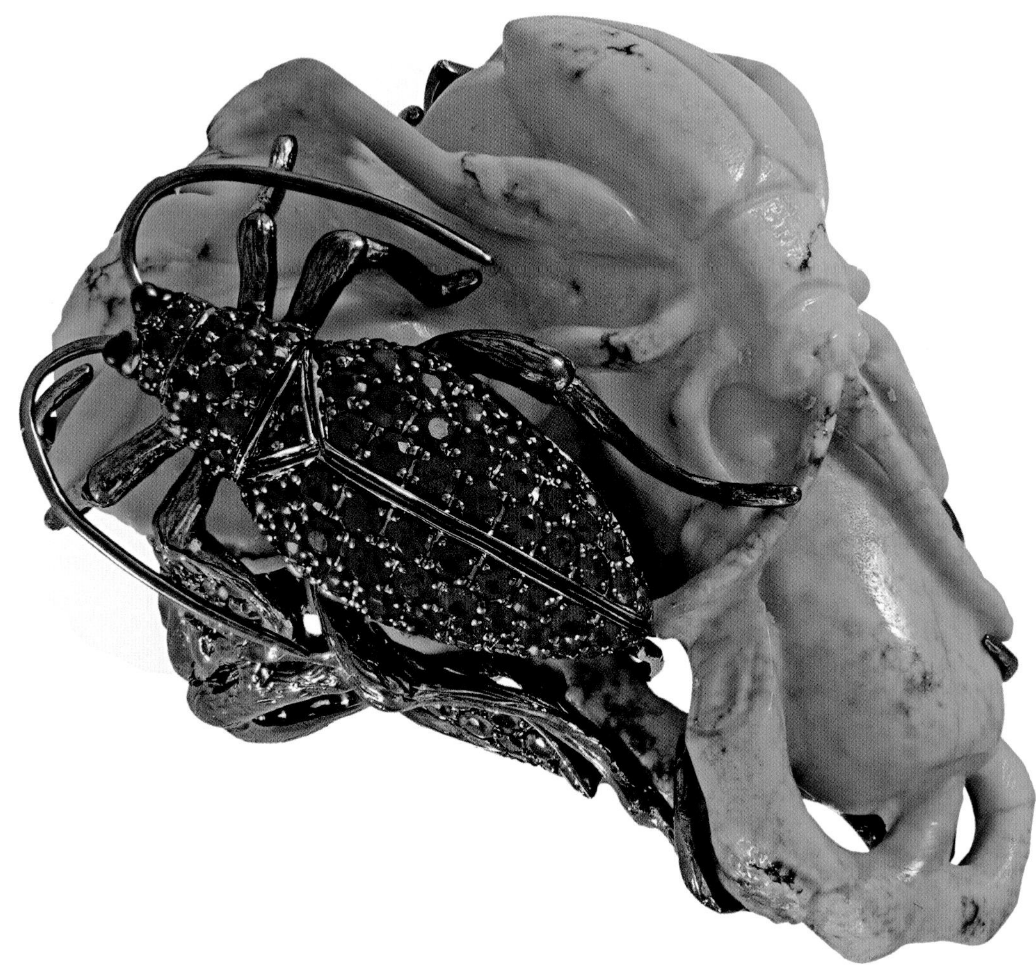

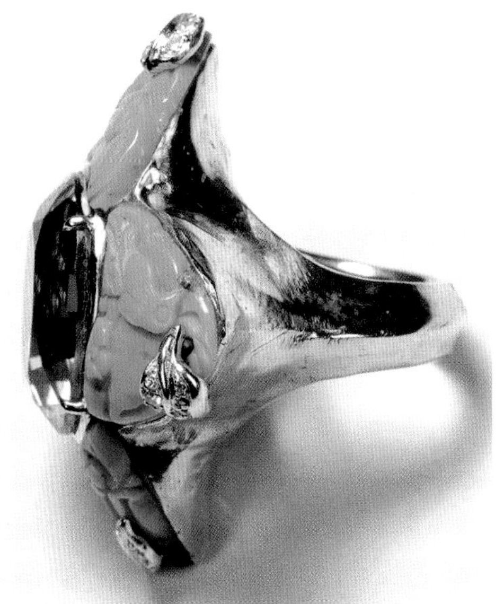

ABOVE:
'COMPASS' RING, c.1998 – AQUAMARINE, CARVED TURQUOISE, DIAMOND, WHITE AND YELLOW GOLD

BELOW:
THREE CARVED PLAQUE RINGS, c.2000 – JADE, GREEN GARNET, TURQUOISE, BLUE TOPAZ, CORAL, ORANGE AND YELLOW SAPPHIRE, WHITE GOLD

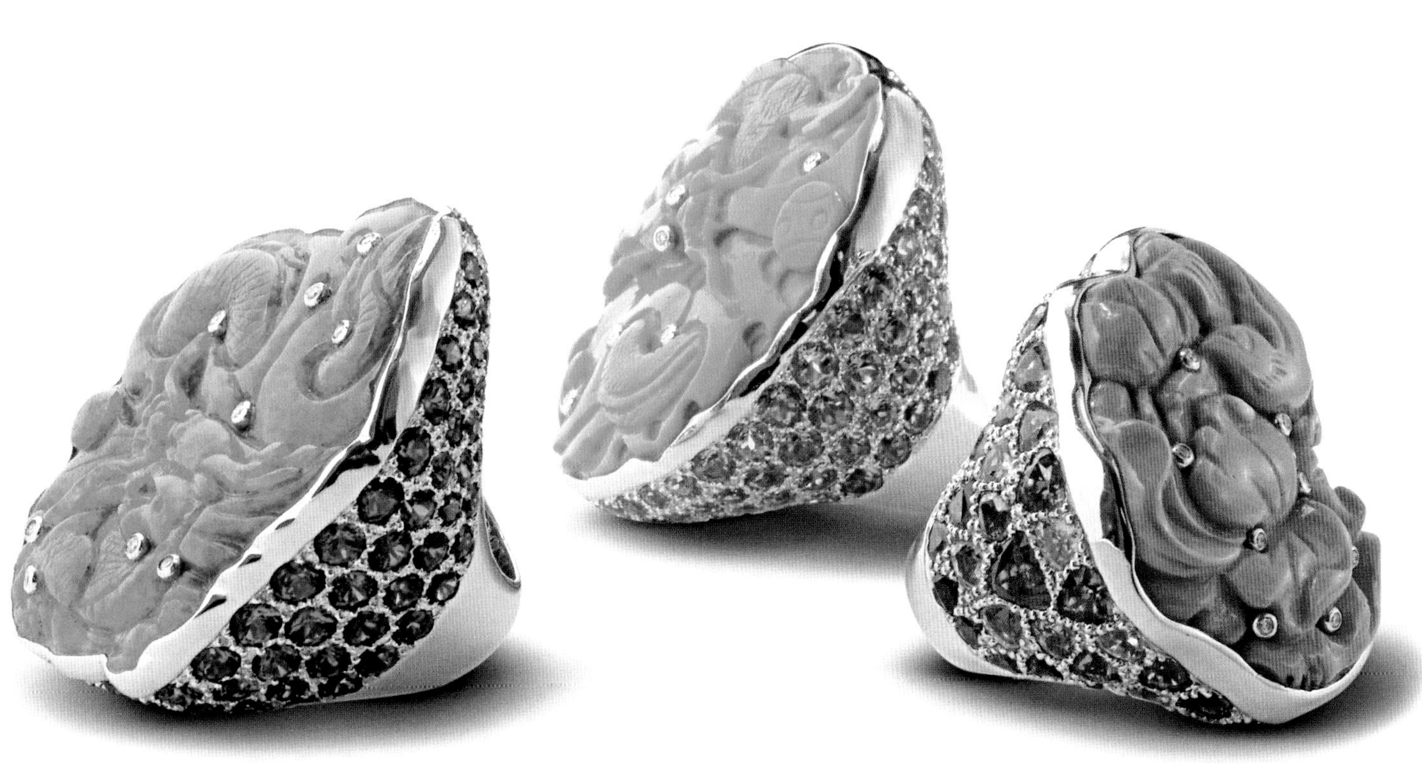

CURIOSITY CABINET

CURIOSITY CABINET – GLYPTIC & CAMEOS – GIVING A NEW LIFE TO FORGOTTEN JEWELS

Popular in the 16th and 17th centuries, the cabinet of curiosities was frequently populated with unusual stuffed animals, birds and insects, shells and unusual objects from antiquity and of historical interest; all lovingly classified. These cabinets were a window to the outside world during a time when few travelled and those who ventured to faraway lands took years to return. This is what made them so important, these wonder rooms, which existed as much to impress as they did to educate; a role that would later be filled by museums.

Lydia Courteille was inspired by these specimen cabinets, including the collection housed in the eclectic museum of the great Egyptologist Sir John Soane. Courteille's own curiosity cabinet holds a collection of large shells, red coral branches, pieces of amber, lava and turquoise, some of which were transformed into huge hoop earrings and massive cocktail rings created from forgotten shell and agate cameos from antiquity and later from the 19th century. Jewelled blackamoor cameos exquisitely carved, adorned with tiny diamonds, rest alongside portraits of the ancient gods.

Delicately painted Limoges enamel portraits in coloured, grey and white enamel on black enamel backgrounds, and liturgical enamel portraits with golden chased backgrounds, such as a Russian *Madonna and Child*, are all a part of Courteille's world. Other oddities include vanities and glyptics, some over 4,000 years old.

Courteille provocatively created bangles using ancient glyptics and set them with messages from the 21st century: the sacred ankh (the ancient Egyptian hieroglyphic symbol of life) and the phrase 'Gala ma Muse' (a reference to Dalí's great love affair with his wife and muse, Gala) come together to shed a tear.

Four-leaf clovers, exotic humming birds, light-winged butterflies, bats and dragonflies are other oddments brought back from travels abroad and her rummagings in the dark corners of bric-à-brac stores and antique shops. These all remind Courteille of a place, an event, a moment in history, or a tale, such as Orpheus and Eurydice in the Underworld.

For many of Courteille's jewels, this Curiosity Cabinet is their first resting post before being placed into another singular collection.

PREVIOUS SPREAD:
THE BALLERINA SNEAKS A PEEK INTO THE 'KUNSTKAMMER', WHERE LYDIA COURTEILLE KEEPS ALL HER UNUSUAL JEWELS, FROM 19TH-CENTURY CAMEOS AND GLYPTICS OF ANOTHER AGE TO SPECIMENS OF BEETLES, INSECTS, BUTTERFLIES AND STARFISH. THIS IS WHERE MANY OF HER JEWELS BEGIN THEIR JOURNEY

Digital image by Natalie Shau

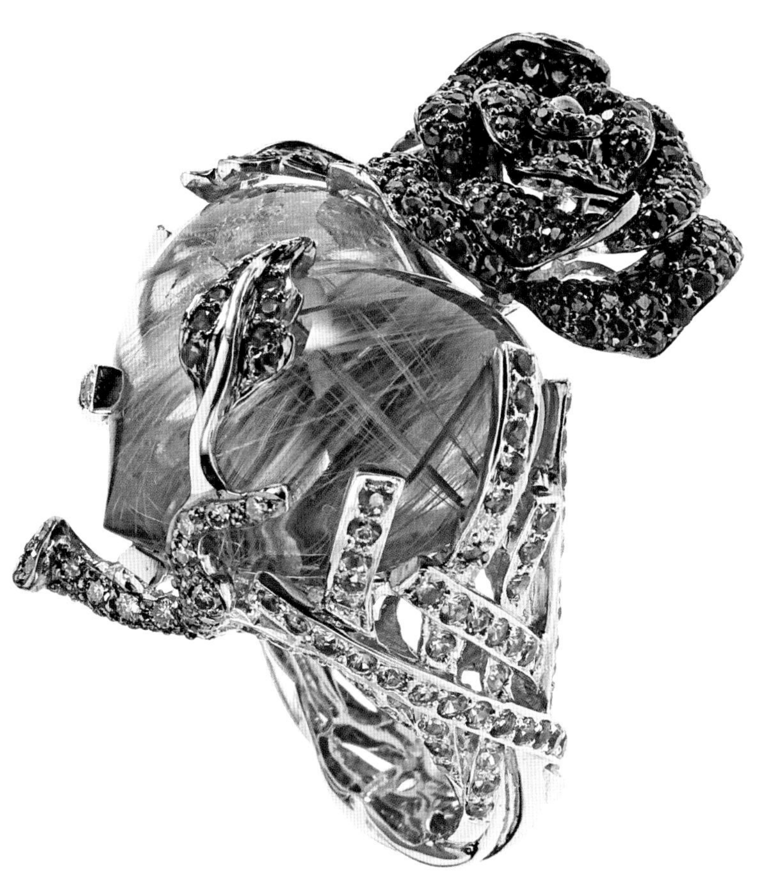

OPPOSITE PAGE, TOP:
BACCHUS RING, c.2004 – CORAL CAMEO, OPAL, WHITE GOLD
Lydia Courteille sets her Bacchus peering through a cloud of sparkling champagne bubbles.

OPPOSITE PAGE, BOTTOM:
INDIAN CHIEF BROOCH/PENDANT, c. 2006 – OPAL, RUBY, DIAMOND, RHODIUM-PLATED GOLD, YELLOW GOLD, PALE PINK ENAMEL
Note the feathers sculpted in the headdress and the sculpted rose at the centre of his breastplate of petals.

ABOVE:
MASK & FEATHER RING, c.2004 – CORAL, DIAMOND, WHITE GOLD

LEFT:
HEART AND ROSE RING – ANGEL HAIR QUARTZ, RUBY, TSAVORITE GARNET, CHAMPAGNE- AND COGNAC-COLOURED DIAMONDS, BLACK RHODIUM-PLATED GOLD, YELLOW GOLD

TOP LEFT:
RUSSIAN 'MADONNA AND CHILD' RING, c.2006 – 19TH-CENTURY RUSSIAN ENAMEL PORTRAIT WITH GOLD CHASED BACKGROUND, DIAMOND, PINK SAPPHIRE, VIOLET ENAMEL FLORETS, YELLOW GOLD

TOP RIGHT:
'RUNNING FOX' CAMEO RING, c.2008 – CHALCEDONY, ROSE-CUT DIAMOND, BLACK RHODIUM-PLATED GOLD

BOTTOM LEFT:
CHERUB CAMEO RING – LAVA, SEED PEARLS, DIAMOND, VIOLET TRANSLUCENT ENAMEL FLORETS, OXIDISED SILVER, YELLOW GOLD

BOTTOM RIGHT:
CHERUB CAMEO AND SNAKE RING – SHELL CAMEO, SAPPHIRE, BLACK RHODIUM-PLATED GOLD

ABOVE:
BLACKAMOOR CAMEO RING, c.2004 – 19TH-CENTURY AGATE CAMEO, CHAMPAGNE-COLOURED DIAMOND, YELLOW GOLD

RIGHT:
LIMOGES ENAMEL PORTRAIT OF A LADY RING, c.2010 – GREEN AND RED TRANSLUCENT ENAMEL, ROSE-CUT DIAMOND, DIAMOND, YELLOW GOLD

TOP LEFT:
'SITTING DOG' MOSAIC RING – ROMAN MOSAIC, CHAMPAGNE-COLOURED DIAMOND, GREEN AND RED ENAMEL, SILVER, YELLOW GOLD

BOTTOM LEFT:
'TOWER' MOSAIC RING – ROMAN MOSAIC, BLACK AND WHITE DIAMOND, YELLOW GOLD

TOP RIGHT:
'ANCIENT SCENE' MOSAIC RING – ROMAN MOSAIC, JASPER, CHAMPAGNE-COLOURED ROSE-CUT DIAMONDS, GREEN ENAMEL, YELLOW GOLD

BOTTOM RIGHT:
'BUTTERFLY' MOSAIC RING – ROMAN MOSAIC, DIAMOND, RUBY, YELLOW GOLD

> *"Paris is a mine of inspiration, from its architecture mixing old with contemporary, its catacombs dating from the 18th century and its antiquities waiting to be discovered in its museums. Its museums are full of treasures and unusual objects – a veritable wonderland tracing the past."*

'STREETS OF PARIS' TIARA – BLACK DIAMOND, RUBY, BLACK RHODIUM-PLATED GOLD, YELLOW GOLD

ABOVE:
BAT RING – DRUZY QUARTZ CRYSTAL, BLACK DIAMOND, RUBY, BLACK RHODIUM-PLATED GOLD

RIGHT:
BAT BRACELET – DRUZY QUARTZ CRYSTAL, COGNAC-COLOURED DIAMOND, RUBY, RHODIUM-PLATED GOLD

ABOVE:
'GALA MA MUSE' BRACELET – ANCIENT EGYPTIAN 'EYE' OF A MUMMY GLYPTIC (5,000 YEARS OLD), DIAMOND, YELLOW GOLD

ABOVE:
'GALA MA MUSE' BRACELET – ANCIENT EGYPTIAN 'EYE' OF A MUMMY GLYPTIC (5,000 YEARS OLD), BLACK DIAMOND, YELLOW GOLD
This is a reference to Salvador Dalí's muse, Gala.

BELOW LEFT AND RIGHT:
ANCIENT EGYPTIAN GLYPTIC RING (TOP AND SIDE VIEWS) – ANCIENT EGYPTIAN AMULET GLYPTIC (5000 YEARS OLD), TSAVORITE GARNET, OPAL, RHODIUM-PLATED GOLD

PUBLICITY IMAGE SHOWING MODEL WEARING CORAL AND DIAMOND JEWELLERY FROM THE 'CURIOSITY CABINET' COLLECTION

Photograph by Marco Latte

SECRET GARDEN

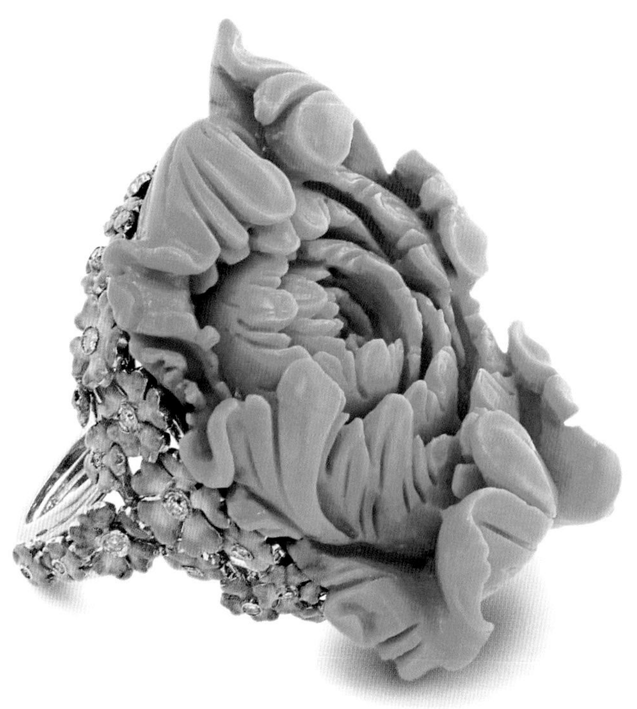

ABOVE LEFT:
PEONY RING – TURQUOISE, PINK AND PALE BLUE ENAMEL FLORETS, DIAMOND, YELLOW GOLD

ABOVE RIGHT:
INSECT RING, c.2005 – MORGANITE, RUBY, EMERALD, CHAMPAGNE-COLOURED DIAMOND, PALE BLUE AND PINK ENAMEL, YELLOW GOLD

OPPOSITE PAGE:
EARLY RING, c.2004 – AQUAMARINE, GREEN GARNET, OPAL, CHAMPAGNE-COLOURED DIAMOND, WHITE DIAMOND, WHITE GOLD

PREVIOUS SPREAD:
JEWELLED FLOWERS AND FRUIT GROW ALONGSIDE EACH OTHER AND SHARE THEIR GARDEN WITH BIRDS, INSECTS AND SPIDERS
Digital image by Natalie Shau

SECRET GARDEN – FLOWERS

The flowers in Courteille's designs take a pragmatic view of nature, they are not perfect, and they are regularly populated by beetles, spiders and other such creepy crawlies. These were some of her first jewellery pieces and she called them her '*Habillage*' (dressed) pieces.

As well as Insects, Courteille somtimes decorates them with jewelled symbols, adding to the mix with their shapes and their outline. There is no fixed interpretation of these pieces: Courteille insists that it is for the wearer to create their own story and meaning for the jewel.

She seeks out the already sculpted gemstones and with her flair, she transforms them. They are in fact jewels that she has 'dressed up' and framed with tiny gemstones.

Flowers were her first jewels and the first flower ring (1990) spent more than two years on a jeweller's bench, struggling to advance to the point of completion. Time passed and so did numerous other people, who saw the ring in progress. The inevitable happened: other designs similar to hers began to appear before she could even recover her own ring from the workshop and present it to the world.

Frustrated, Courteille learnt the first of many difficult lessons in the world of jewellery – if she wanted to stop others from copying her, she had to move forward, to design and produce new ideas continuously, just to stay ahead. This was the advice of Karl Lagerfeld when she asked him how he was able to accept this phenomenon.

From these tentative beginnings, Courteille created her first collection of jewellery; it was 1998.

LEFT:
PEONY RING, c.2005 – ANGEL SKIN CORAL, BLACK ENAMEL, RUBY, CHAMPAGNE-COLOURED DIAMOND, BLACK DIAMOND, BLACK RHODIUM-PLATED GOLD

BELOW LEFT:
DRAGONFLY EARRINGS, c.2008 – AMETHYST, SAPPHIRE, BLUE ENAMEL, BLACK RHODIUM-PLATED GOLD

BELOW RIGHT:
DRAGONFLY EARRINGS – AMETHYST, RUBY, SAPPHIRE, DIAMOND, YELLOW GOLD

ABOVE LEFT:
EARLY FLOWER RING, c.2000 – AQUAMARINE, AMETHYST, GREEN GARNET, DIAMOND, WHITE GOLD

ABOVE RIGHT:
HIBISCUS RING – YELLOW AND ORANGE SAPPHIRES, GARNET, BLACK RHODIUM-PLATED GOLD, YELLOW GOLD

LEFT:
ORCHID RING – SUGELITE, RUBY, BLACK RHODIUM-PLATED GOLD

OPPOSITE PAGE:
FROG NECKLACE AND EARRINGS – CARVED JADE PLAQUES, RUBY, GREEN GARNET, BLACK RHODIUM-PLATED GOLD
Special order for Lane Crawford, Hong Kong

RIGHT:
ROSE RING – ANGEL SKIN CORAL, TSAVORITE GARNET, DIAMOND, WHITE GOLD

BELOW LEFT:
ROSE AND BAT RING, c.2004 – RED CORAL, SPINEL, RUBY, DIAMOND, BLACK RHODIUM-PLATED GOLD
This ring is the link between the 'Secret Garden' collection and the 'Bestiary' collection.

BELOW RIGHT:
POPPY AND DRAGON FLY RING, c.2000 – RED CORAL, DIAMOND, BLACK RHODIUM-PLATED GOLD

BESTIARY

ABOVE:
PRINCE CHARMING RING, c.2006 – PINK SAPPHIRE, EMERALD, DIAMOND, BLACK RHODIUM-PLATED GOLD, GOLD

OPPOSITE PAGE, TOP LEFT:
BAT RING – RUBELLITE, PINK SAPPHIRE, BLACK RHODIUM-PLATED GOLD

OPPOSITE PAGE, CENTRE:
COILING SNAKE BRACELET – RUBY, DIAMOND, GOLD

OPPOSITE PAGE, TOP RIGHT:
BAT CREOLE HOOP EARRINGS – PINK SAPPHIRE, BLACK RHODIUM-PLATED GOLD

PREVIOUS SPREAD:
THE VEILED BEAUTY WEARS SNAKES, BATS AND MONKEYS ON HER ARM. THEY ARE ALL AMBASSADORS IN LYDIA COURTEILLE'S COLLECTION, WHICH IS POPULATED WITH INSECTS, FROGS AND REPTILES AS WELL AS BIRDS AND UNUSUAL CREATURES FROM LYDIA COURTEILLE'S IMAGINATION
Digital image by Natalie Shau

BESTIARY (2006)

Courteille's zoological garden spills over with jewelled bugs, serpents, monkeys, frogs, darting bats, moths and dragonflies; salamanders catch winged insects, whilst mythological dragons breathe their wisdom and alligators attack and devour their prey.

Courteille shows Earth's creatures in their natural state: cruel and unsentimental. From winged imaginary beasts to her skeletal sirens and beetles, they embrace pools of coloured gemstones – bats with outspread wings; serpents bestowing their source of knowledge on unusual gemstones, protecting, with their coils, the edges of delicately carved petals.

Interested in the various meanings bestowed on animals from one part of the world to another, Courteille's world of dragons, bats and snakes are used to emphasise the cultural differences and symbolic meanings in the West and in the East; creatures of good fortune in the East, can conjure up images of malevolence in the West.

Serpents are a favourite motif. Courteille loves their versatility and their multi-layered meanings as *memento mori*: in The Old Testament, the snake is generally a symbol of evil – the serpent who tempts Adam to eat the fruit of the Tree of Knowledge of Good and Evil in the Garden of Eden – though also as a symbol of healing – the bronze serpent Moses mounted on a staff to cure people from snake bites in the Book of Numbers. In ancient Chinese lore, the snake is cunning, wise and beautiful, it is contrastingly considered as one of the five noxious creatures (*wu du*) to be driven out on the fifth day of the fifth month of the Chinese lunar calendar, which happens to be the beginning of Summer and also the day of the Duanwu Festival (the Dragon Boat festival) or it is associated with the dragon and revered as auspicious, bringing luck and good harvest; whilst in Greek mythology, they are the source of wisdom and healing – the rod of Ascelpius is the symbol of Western medicine to this day.

Courteille's creatures climb up creole earrings; and monkeys clamber over angel skin coral peach blossoms, inspired by the porcelain from the Yongzheng and Qianlong periods, which depicted the Monkey King (Sun Wukong) stealing peaches of eternal life in the great Ming dynasty Chinese novel, *Journey to the West*. Images of bats eating peaches on porcelain from the same period symbolise fertility, the springtime and a long life; though bats are not looked upon with tenderness in the West, they are auspicious creatures in the East. Courteille enjoys these contradictions and she is at pains to highlight and contrast these incongruities in her work, provoking reflection and creating awareness

TOP LEFT:
ROSE AND MONKEY RING – ANGEL SKIN CORAL, TSAVORITE GARNET, CHAMPAGNE-COLOURED DIAMOND, BLACK & WHITE DIAMOND, BLACK RHODIUM-PLATED GOLD, GOLD

TOP RIGHT:
'MONKEY LOOKING INTO THE FUTURE' RING – ROCK CRYSTAL, CHAMPAGNE- AND COGNAC-COLOURED DIAMONDS, WHITE DIAMOND, BLACK RHODIUM-PLATED TEXTURED GOLD, TEXTURED YELLOW GOLD

Etched into the crystal ball is an image of Charles Darwin.

RIGHT:
MONKEY AND SERPENT CREOLE EARRINGS – GREEN TURQUOISE, TSAVORITE GARNET, CHAMPAGNE-COLOURED DIAMOND, BLACK RHODIUM-PLATED GOLD

TOP LEFT:
MONKEY CREOLE HOOP EARRINGS – ONYX, CORAL, DIAMOND, WHITE GOLD

TOP RIGHT:
BUTTERFLY CREOLE HOOP EARRINGS – TSAVORITE GARNET, DIAMOND, BLACK RHODIUM-PLATED GOLD

LEFT:
SERPENT CREOLE HOOP EARRINGS, c.2003 – CHAMPAGNE-COLOURED DIAMOND, ONYX, WHITE GOLD

BAT AND PEACH BRACELET, c.2006 – WHITE CORAL, TSAVORITE GARNET, RUBY, CHAMPAGNE-COLOURED DIAMOND, BLACK RHODIUM-PLATED GOLD

In Chinese mythology, the monkey symbolises longevity; when it is portrayed with peaches (a symbol of immortality), it becomes a blessing for a long life.

BAT EAR PENDANTS, c.2006 – RUBY, PEARL, CHAMPAGNE-COLOURED DIAMOND, GOLD

BELOW:
CROCODILE EATING PREY RING – EMERALD, TSAVORITE GARNET, CHAMPAGNE-COLOURED DIAMOND, BLACK RHODIUM-PLATED GOLD, GOLD

OPPOSITE PAGE, TOP:
CROCODILE RING – PARAIBA TOURMALINE, TSAVORITE GARNET, BLACK DIAMOND, BLACK RHODIUM-PLATED GOLD

OPPOSITE PAGE, BOTTOM
CROCODILE AND SNAKE RING – PARAIBA TOURMALINE, TSAVORITE GARNET, RUBY, DIAMOND, BLACK RHODIUM-PLATED GOLD, GOLD

MARACAIBO (2013)

Inspiration for this collection came in part from Cartier's magnificent double crocodile necklace for Mexican film actress, María Félix in the 1970s.

Using clear bright turquoise Paraiba tourmalines, Courteille tries to capture the Catacumba lightning flashes of the huge Maracaibo estuary. She depicts alligators in their natural state: catching other creatures for food, fighting for dominance, or just sunbathing with their huge jaws open.

These jewels serve to remind the wearer of the fragile distinctive beauty of Lake Maracaibo and to the endangered species living along its shores. This large turquoise, fresh-water lagoon, populated with wildlife and fish, meets the Gulf of Venezuela (and beyond to the Caribbean Sea) via the Tablazo Strait. Widening of the strait to allow larger ships to pass through and oil production in the surrounding basin are changing the region's eco-system.

In the past, it was used as a haunt for pirates taking refuge from patrolling naval vessels. Stilt villages have lived undisturbed for years in harmony with the surrounding swamps and the Perijá mountain ranges.

But for how long will this idyll last?

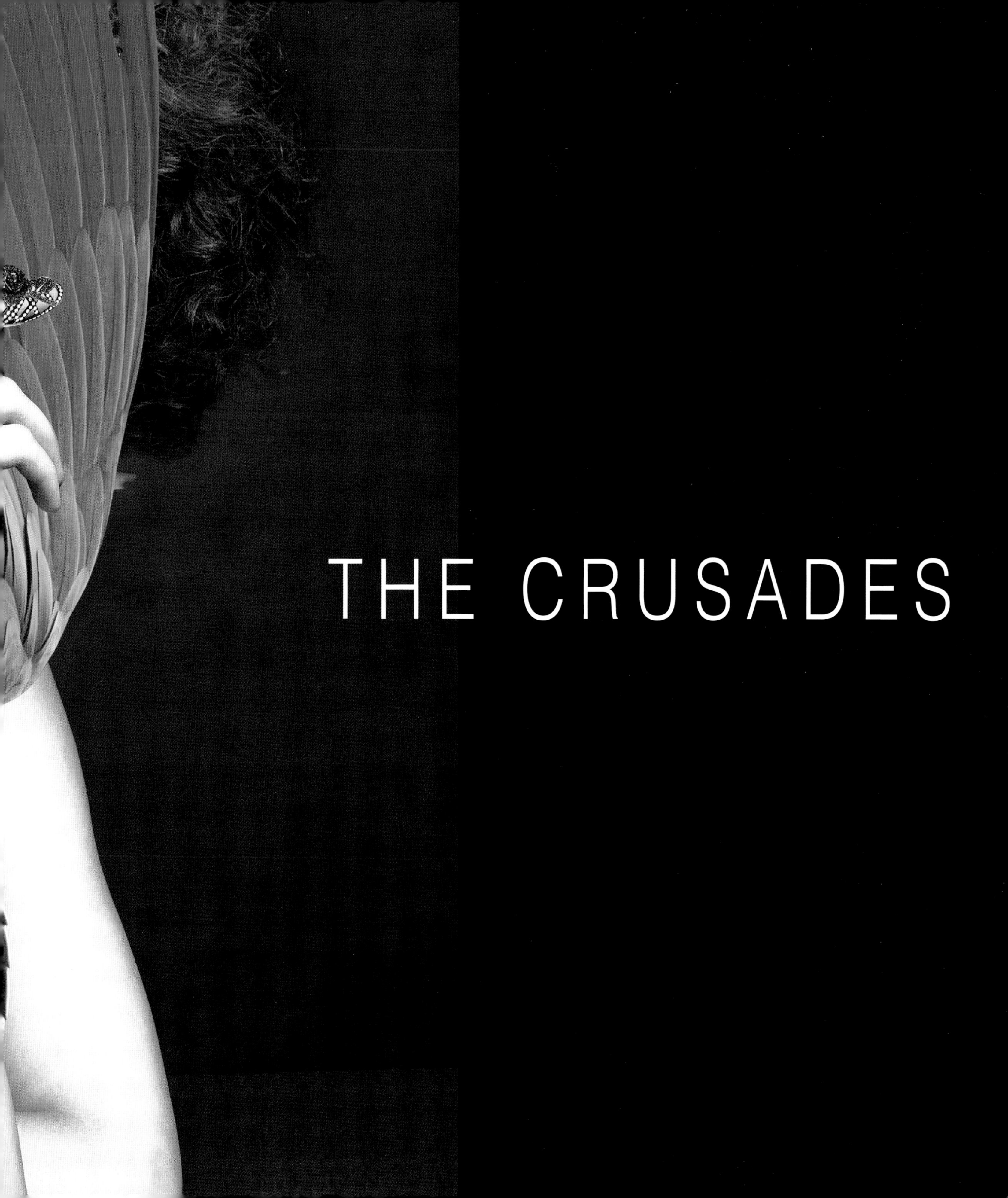

THE CRUSADES

PREVIOUS SPREAD:
THE WINGED ANGEL WEARS THE REGALIA OF THE KNIGHTS FROM THE CRUSADES WITH MASONIC AND RELIGIOUS SYMBOLS. LYDIA COURTEILLE'S JEWELS ARE GIVEN AN IMMEDIACY AND A CONTEMPORARY TOUCH BY TRANSFORMING BIKER RINGS INTO FINGER RINGS AND MARRYING THEM WITH IMAGES OF THE ARCHANGEL GABRIEL AND ICONS FROM OTHER CULTURES, SUCH AS A DIAMOND DRAGON FROM THE EAST OR ROSES, WHICH GIVE A TOUCH OF FEMININITY
Digital image by Natalie Shau

OPPOSITE PAGE:
WINGED SWORD EARRINGS – SAPPHIRE, DIAMOND, WHITE GOLD

LEFT:
ANGEL EXTERMINATOR BIKER RING – SAPPHIRE, DIAMOND, WHITE GOLD

THE CRUSADES – SYMBOLISM

The Crusades were an important element in Medieval European history; they were the wars of religion waged well before those of the 16th century. Knights in armour wielding swords, horses dressed in chainmail and caparisons, fighting against an equally fervent army of Saracens defending their hold on the Holy Lands. The Crusades conjure up images of knights from the Teutonic and Livonian orders and the Knights Templar of the Middle Ages.

Emblems of valour, divine protection, honour and courage mix with those of fidelity, chivalry, nobility and fleet of foot. This early collection is an expression for Courteille's love of history and it was inspired by her admiration for *Les Rois maudits* by Maurice Druon. This series of seven historical novels tells the story of the French monarchy from King Philip IV of France (Philippe le Bel) and begins with the arrests of the Knights Templar and the burning at the stake of the Grand Master Jacques de Molay. At his death, Jacques de Molay is said to have cursed Philip IV and his descendents as well as Guillaume de Nogaret and the Pope Clement V, who had played pivotal roles in the trial of the Knights Templar. Within three years they were all dead.

The 'Crusades' collection has had a significant influence on Courteille's later collections and it has also provided ideas for many of her 'transversal' jewels, which travel through her many collections, linking them together one by one. Fatima's hand, the Latin cross, and masonic emblems, have all found a home in this collection.

The outlines of symbolic images, both religious and secular, and their multiple meanings intrigue Courteille; she does not profess to any religion, quite deliberately so, she wants the wearer to create their own story. Courteille uses the shapes of these images and the sense of history, to create a multi-layered duality in her jewels.

Again, East meets that of the West: the auspicious dragon of the East meets its fate at the hands of Saint George and Saint Michael in Western lore. Using these elements, Courteille gives the collection a modern-day reference by transforming her 'knights in shining armour' into biker rings.

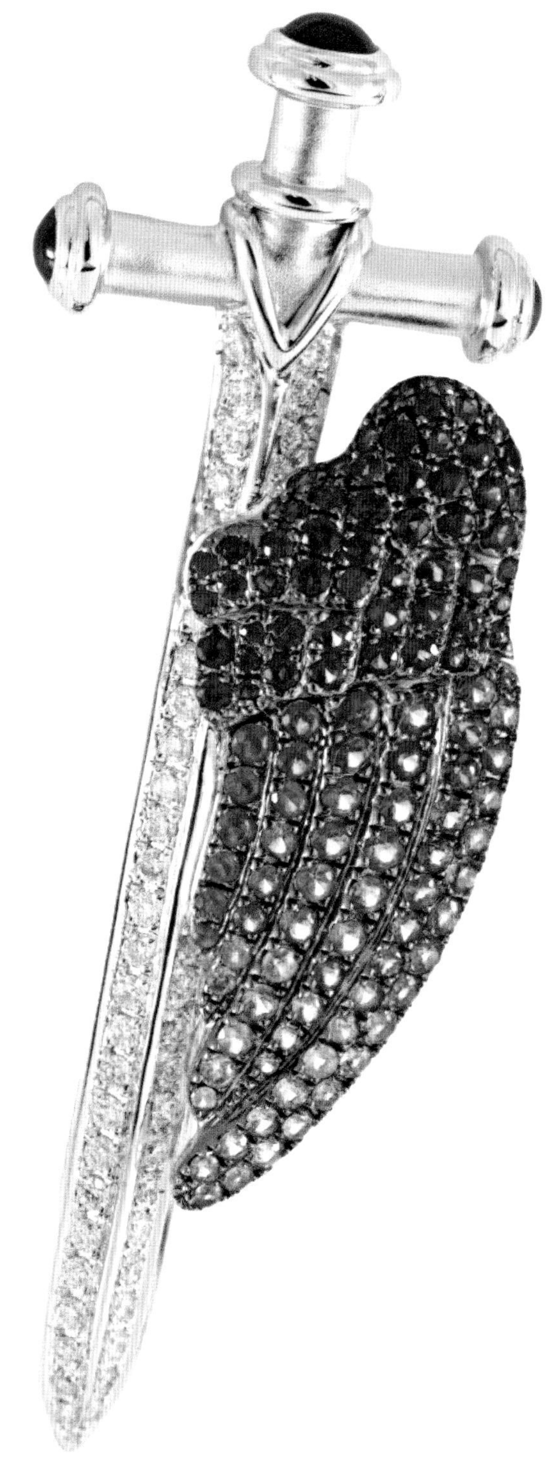

ABOVE:

KNIGHT'S HELMET EARRINGS – CHAMPAGNE-COLOURED DIAMOND, WHITE DIAMOND, BLACK RHODIUM-PLATED GOLD, GOLD

TOP RIGHT:

SHIELD RING – WHITE AND BLACK DIAMONDS, BLACK RHODIUM-PLATED GOLD

RIGHT:

ARMOUR BIKER RING – DIAMOND, BLACK RHODIUM-PLATED GOLD, WHITE GOLD

Courteille's duality is a feature of this ring: the Chinese mythological dragon meets Western 20th-century Harley Davidson biker culture.

OPPOSITE PAGE:

SAINT MICHAEL BY RAPHAEL (SANZIO RAFFAELLO, 1483-1520), c.1505

Paris, musée du Louvre; Photograph © RMN-Grand Palais (musée du Louvre) / Tony Querrec

INRI
I.N R.I

AUTODAFÉ

AUTODAFÉ – 'CHAOS IN THE CEMETERY'

ABOVE:
'BUDDHA'S FEET DECORATED WITH A LOTUS FLOWER' RING – TSAVORITE GARNET, PURPLE SAPPHIRE, RUBY, BLACK RHODIUM-PLATED GOLD, GOLD

OPPOSITE PAGE, TOP LEFT:
ANGEL RING – ANGEL HAIR QUARTZ, BLACK AND WHITE DIAMOND, BLACK RHODIUM-PLATED GOLD

OPPOSITE PAGE, RIGHT:
HEART AND DAGGER RING, c.2002 – GARNET, RUBY, CHAMPAGNE-COLOURED DIAMOND, BLACK DIAMOND, GOLD

OPPOSITE PAGE, BOTTOM LEFT:
CRYSTAL AUTODAFÉ RING – QUARTZ CRYSTAL, BLACK AND WHITE DIAMOND, BLACK RHODIUM-PLATED GOLD

The 'Autodafé / Acte de Foi' collection (Act of Faith) resulted from Courteille's study into Christianity and its symbols, and followed on from the 'Crusades' collection. She mixes her present day experiences with those of the past and refuses to shy away from the many disturbing and uncomfortable questions that arise when one looks back into history. In France, references to the Crusades date back to the 11th century and Courteille makes many references to the knights who left their families to deliver Christ's tomb in Jerusalem, in the holy wars against the Saracens.

The collection is also a reference to the Act of Faith imposed on the Jewish communities by the Spanish Inquisition during the reign of Queen Isabella I. There are many references to this period and at the centre of this collection is the rigidity and cruelty of those past Christian beliefs. Those Jews who would not change to the Catholic faith were burnt at the stake; many fled to Armenia and Turkey seeking a safe haven.

From witch burning, the burning of heretics and its evident connotations of medieval practices, Courteille mixes cultural beliefs with those of history. Never comfortable and never pleasant, Courteille transforms their symbols into controversial, thought-provoking jewels that make the wearer reflect on the past and its relevance to the present.

Courteille is deeply moved by the faith of peoples; a visit that particularly affected her was in Lithuania to the 'Hill of Crosses' to the north of Šiauliai. A place of pilgrimage, Catholics would go to lay a cross and to remember those who had rebelled against Russia in the 1831 and 1863 rebellions and then under the occupation of the Soviet Union in the 20th century. It has become a place of peaceful protest where pilgrims can remember their culture and faith and remains a special memorial for all those who wish to pray. Courteille has used the Latin Cross in many of her jewels.

PREVIOUS SPREAD:
HILL OF CROSSES, LITHUANIA

Natalie

A CASSANDRE

A CASSANDRE – BREVITY, YOUTH AND BEAUTY

In 1552, Ronsard published his *Amours de Cassandre*, dedicated to the fresh beauty of Cassandre Salviati; she was just 13 and Ronsard 20, when they first met in 1545. Ronsard laments the passing of time, of youth and beauty lost; his pink rose illustrates the loss of beauty.

A Cassandre by Pierre Ronsard (1524-1585)

Mignonne, allons voir si la rose Qui ce matin avoitdesclose Sa robe de pourpre au soleil, A point perdu cette vesprée Les plis de sa robe pourprée, Et son teint au vostre pareil.	Sweetheart, let's see if the rose That this morning had open Its purple dress to the Sun, This evening hasn't lost The folds of its purple dress, And its complexion akin to thine.
Las! voiés comme en peu d'espace, Mignonne, elle a dessus la place Las! las, ses beautés laissé cheoir! O vraiment maratre Nature, Puis qu'une telle fleur ne dure Que du matin jusques au soir.	Ah! See how in such a short space My sweetheart, it has on this very spot All its beauties lost! O, so un-motherly Nature, Since such a beautiful flower Only lasts from dawn to dusk!
Donc, si vous me croiés, mignonne : Tandis que vôtre âge fleuronne En sa plus verte nouveauté, Cueillés, cueillés vôtre jeunesse Comme à cette fleur, la vieillesse Fera ternir vôtre beauté.	So if you believe me, my sweetheart: While time still flowers for you, In its freshest novelty, Take, take advantage of your youthful bloom As it did to this flower, the doom Of age will blight your beauty.*

PREVIOUS SPREAD:
FEMININITY WITH ATTITUDE. BEAUTY LASTS FOR BUT A MOMENT, ROSES ARE BRIGHT PINK SAPPHIRES AND RUBIES; BEWARE THE THORNS. RAMBLING ROSES TRANSFORM BIKER RINGS INTO FINGER RINGS AND LATIN CROSSES BECOME OVERGROWN

Digital image by Natalie Shau

BELOW:
LATIN CROSS RING – RUBY, GREEN TURQUOISE, TSAVORITE GARNET, CHAMPAGNE-COLOURED DIAMOND, BLACK RHODIUM-PLATED GOLD

Courteille takes her cue from Ronsard and uses the symbol of the rose to show the brevity and fragility of this beauty. She also recalls how Cassandra, in spite of her beauty and youth, was condemned to be a doomsayer, predicting the future but never to be believed. The French expression "*jouer les Cassandre*" (lit. to play Cassandra, ie. to be a doomsayer) has always intrigued Courteille; it is based on the ancient Greek legend of Cassandra, the daughter of Priam, the King of Troy. The legend tells of how Apollo gives Cassandra the gift of foretelling the future. However, when she refuses his advances, Apollo curses her, so that no-one will believe her prophesies. She foretells the Trojan

*Translation by Camille Chevalier-Karfis, via FrenchToday.com

> “If we can make people dream through the collections, then we have achieved our goal.”

ABOVE:
RONSARD, OEUVRES COMPLETES. IV, ED. LAUMONIER, PARIS, MARCEL DIDIER, 1958-1975

War, but fails to convince her brother Paris not to go to Sparta. When Paris returns to Troy with the beautiful Helen, again the people of Troy ignore Cassandra's warnings.

The poem is very personal to Courteille; she remembers learning Ronsard's poem at primary school. Thus, Cassandra is a part of Courteille's childhood, of Courteille's personal world: '*à Cassandre*', ensnared perhaps, in roses and briars.

The 'A Cassandre' collection was a first look at trying different colours and Courteille took the rose's beauty and provocatively contrasted it with a biker, 'bad girl' theme and tattoo-like imagery. Bright pink sapphire roses abound, ensnaring the jewels of this contradictory collection.

ABOVE:
ROSE EARRINGS – RUBY, PINK SAPPHIRE, TSAVORITE GARNET, TEXTURED BLACK RHODIUM-PLATED GOLD

LEFT:
FINGER RING, c.2007 – RUBY, PINK SAPPHIRE, TSAVORITE GARNET, CHAMPAGNE-COLOURED DIAMOND, WHITE DIAMOND, BLACK RHODIUM-PLATED GOLD, GOLD

OPPOSITE PAGE:
ROSE NECKLACE c.2010 – TSAVORITE GARNET, DIAMOND, TEXTURED GREY RHODIUM-PLATED GOLD

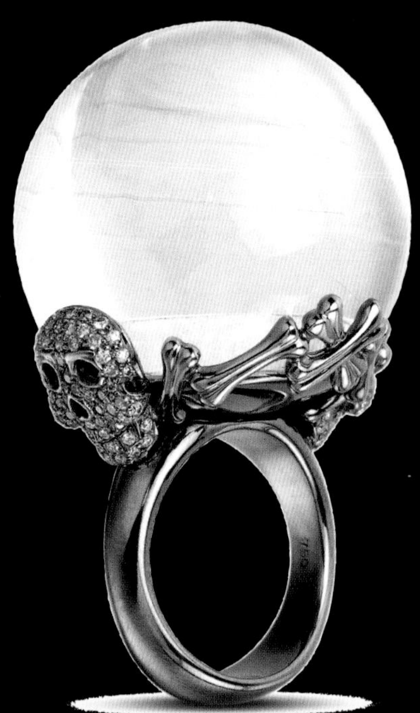
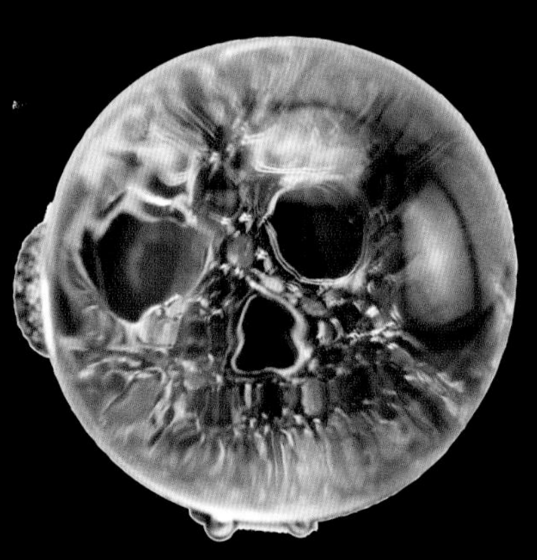

VANITAS
Natalie Shaw

ABOVE:
'VANITAS AND SERPENT' RING – TAHITIAN PEARL, TSAVORITE GARNET, DIAMOND, BLACK RHODIUM-PLATED GOLD

RIGHT:
'MEMENTO MORI' PENDANT, c.2010 – CHAMPAGNE-COLOURED DIAMOND, WHITE DIAMOND, BLACK RHODIUM-PLATED GOLD

OPPOSITE PAGE:
'VANITAS AND SERPENT' EARRINGS – TAHITIAN PEARL, TSAVORITE GARNET, DIAMOND, BLACK RHODIUM-PLATED GOLD

PREVIOUS SPREAD, TOP LEFT:
VANITAS RING – FACETED ROCK CRYSTAL, CHAMPAGNE COLOURED DIAMOND, BLACK RHODIUM-PLATED GOLD

PREVIOUS SPREAD, CENTRE:
'KALEIDOSCOPE VANITAS' RING (SIDE AND TOP VIEW) – ROCK CRYSTAL, CHAMPAGNE-COLOURED DIAMOND, BLACK RHODIUM-PLATED GOLD
The rock crystal for this ring was bought in Namibia, Lydia Courteille was attracted to its kaleidoscopic effect.

PREVIOUS SPREAD, RIGHT:
THIS IS ONE OF LYDIA COURTEILLE'S MOST ENDURING COLLECTIONS. THE VANITAS INVITES US TO REFLECT ON OUR LIVES AND TO REALISE THAT THE PASSAGE OF TIME STOPS FOR NO ONE – BEAUTY IS FLEETING. SHOWN HERE ARE THE TRADITIONAL SYMBOLS OF THE HOURGLASS, THE DELICATE BUTTERFLY AND THE WITHERING FLOWERS
Digital image by Natalie Shau

"Remember death."

VANITAS/MEMENTO MORI

A diamond skeleton walks across the lapis lazuli globe, reminding us of wars that have torn peoples and cultures apart, a flicker of a second, in the history of the world. He is the witness to the births, weddings, and successes too; the simple joys of families and the inevitable passing of one generation to the next...

Vanitas were popular In antiquity: medicines were rudimentary; pestilence, death in childbirth and war were common companions; and people rarely lived beyond the age of 50. Perhaps it was understandable, then, that people were so preoccupied with death.

Legend tells how during victory marches, Roman Emperors and Generals would have slaves whisper "*Memento mori*" to them, to remind them of their mortality. Skulls, reminders of the inevitability of death, were an invitation to reflect on the course of one's life and mortality; they made people reflect on morality and the health of the soul and it was hoped that they would invoke humility.

For centuries, *memento mori* were a part of life, in fashion and in mourning. Now, by the beginning of the 21st century, they have become more of a fashion statement. Death

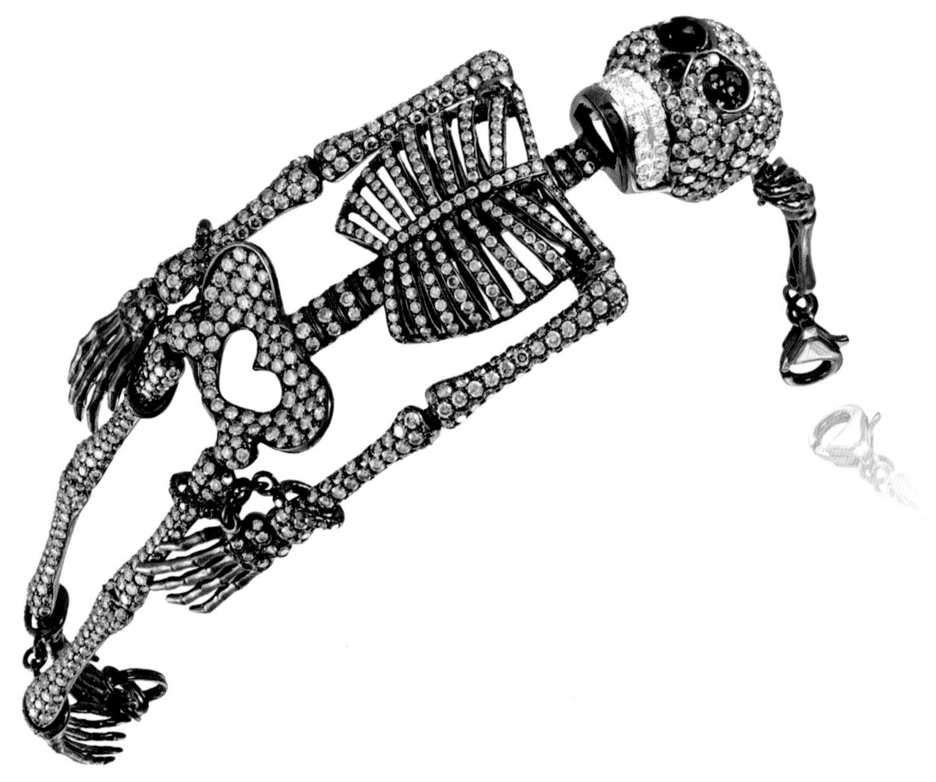

is no longer considered, no longer reflected upon, death is no longer welcome in the homes of the Western world.

Courteille has been collecting *memento mori* since the very beginning of her career. Her fascination for them was confirmed in 1998 when a friend, the writer and producer Nathalie Rheims and an Italian collector of Codognato jewels from Venice asked Courteille to create a ring using a skull form as the central piece; they wanted to try something different and asked Courteille to add her magic touch to such a ring. Courteille took up the challenge and thus her long relationship with pieces that suggest the brevity of life and the unstoppable march of time, began in earnest. Courteille's *memento mori* have become her most recognisable signature. It is a philosophy that reminds you that you can be rich, intelligent and beautiful, but that in the end, everyone has the same destiny.

Courteille revisits *memento mori* in both her 'Catacombs' and 'Bravery' collections. In 'Catacombs', she recalls the tragedy of massacres and of those moments in history when epidemics and fever took hold of whole cities and the corpses were placed in catacombs to avoid the spread of disease – their skeletons now a reminder of their dreadful fate and yet also proof that they once existed. Félicien Rops' drawings were a particular inspiration.

'Bravery' is about the blindness of men in war – "*La mort, la mort, la mort.*" (Death, death, death).

On a more frivolous and humorous note, *memento mori* also make an appearance in Courteille's 'Pirates' collection, à la Johnny Depp in the *Pirates of the Caribbean* films.

Courteille's vanitas jewels have a certain insouciance, a casual indifference, whilst swinging from earlobes, reclining in diamond moons (an ironic suggestion for the man in the moon), whilst others are ear clips transformed from lucky four-leaf clovers to the skull and cross bones of the 'Jolly Roger'.

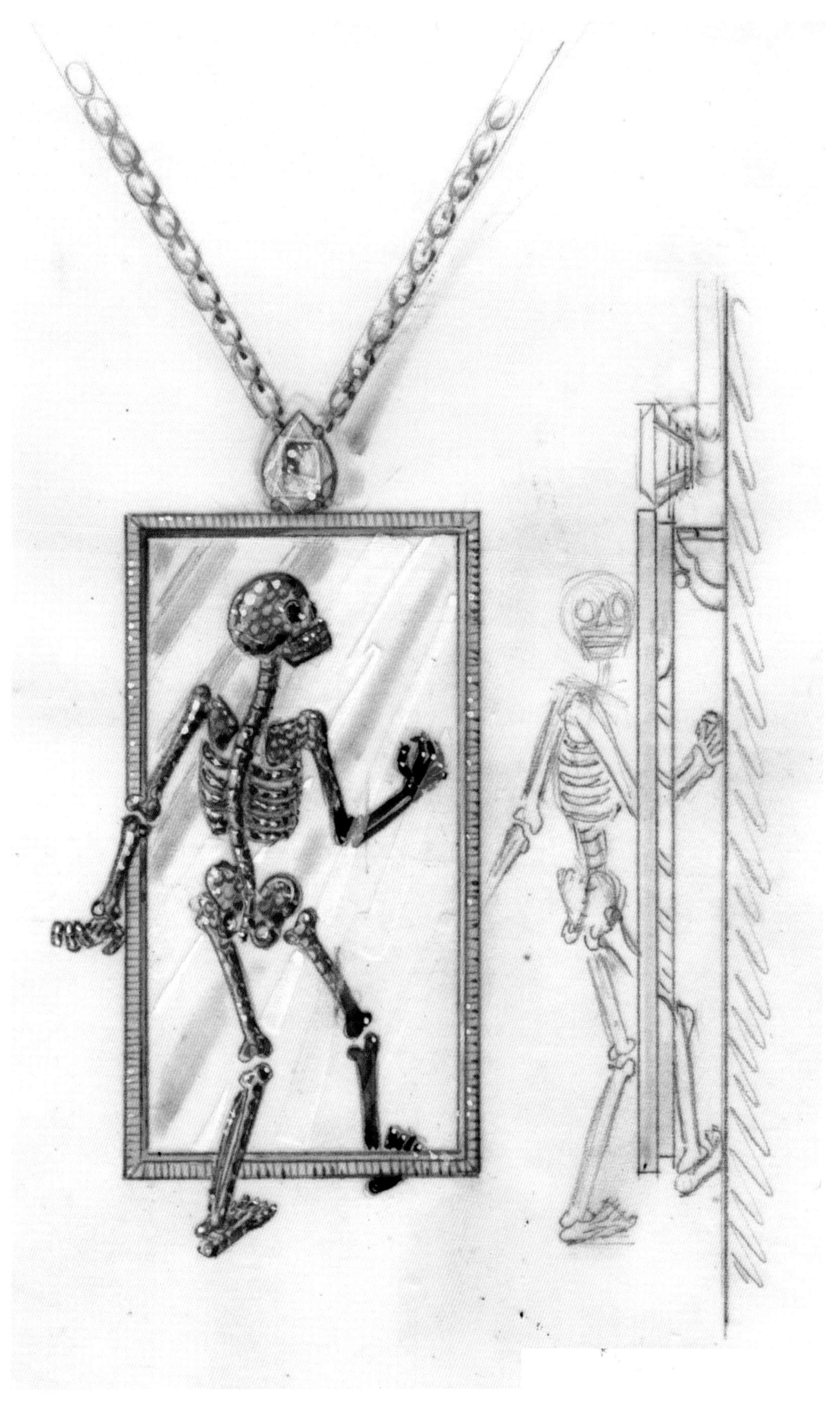

ABOVE:
A 'MEMENTO MORI COUPLE' PENDANT/BROOCH, c.2007 – BOULDER OPAL, DIAMOND, WHITE GOLD

RIGHT:
'MEMENTO MORI WALKING ACROSS THE WORLD' PENDANT, c.2010 – LAPIS LAZULI, DIAMOND, WHITE GOLD

OPPOSITE PAGE:
GOUACHE OF MEMENTO MORI SLIPPING BACK INTO THE PAST FROM THE PRESENT, EARLY 2012

Gouache by Armelle Fontaine.

ABOVE:
'VANITAS IN THE STARS' RING – SAPPHIRE, DIAMOND, BLACK RHODIUM-PLATED GOLD, GOLD

RIGHT:
'MASKED VANITAS' RING – SAPPHIRE, BLACK AND WHITE DIAMOND, BLACK RHODIUM-PLATED GOLD, GOLD

OPPOSITE PAGE:
PIRATE 'SKULL AND CROSS BONE' VANITAS CHAIN – CHAMPAGNE-COLOURED DIAMOND, BLACK RHODIUM-PLATED GOLD

BRAVERY (2008)

Courteille is making a political statement to wake up the wearer and onlooker to the pitfalls of being blindly led by politicians into wars and predicaments that have no meaning.

Her vanities are swathed in their national flags – blinded, unseeing and incapable of individual thought, her vanities are led into war by a sense of nationalism that can be manipulated by the powers that be. With the Stars and Stripes, Courteille was thinking of the Vietnam War; the French flag was a reminder of the crisis in Algeria and the conflicts in the Far East; the Union Jack was a reminder of the Falklands War in the 1980s. Her witty portrayal of each nation's Achilles' heel, gives the jewels in this collection an extra poignancy.

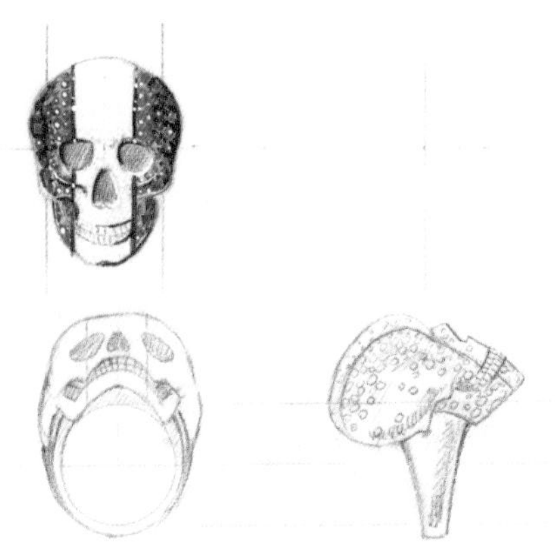

ABOVE:
GOUACHE DESIGN FOR THE FRENCH TRI-COLOUR VANITAS WITH FRONT AND SIDE VIEWS
Gouache and drawing by Armelle Fontaine

BELOW LEFT:
FRENCH TRICOLORE VANITAS RING – RUBY, SAPPHIRE, DIAMOND, BLACK RHODIUM-PLATED GOLD, WHITE GOLD

BELOW RIGHT:
CHINESE RED FLAG VANITAS RING – RUBY, DEEP YELLOW SAPPHIRE, BLACK RHODIUM-PLATED GOLD, WHITE GOLD

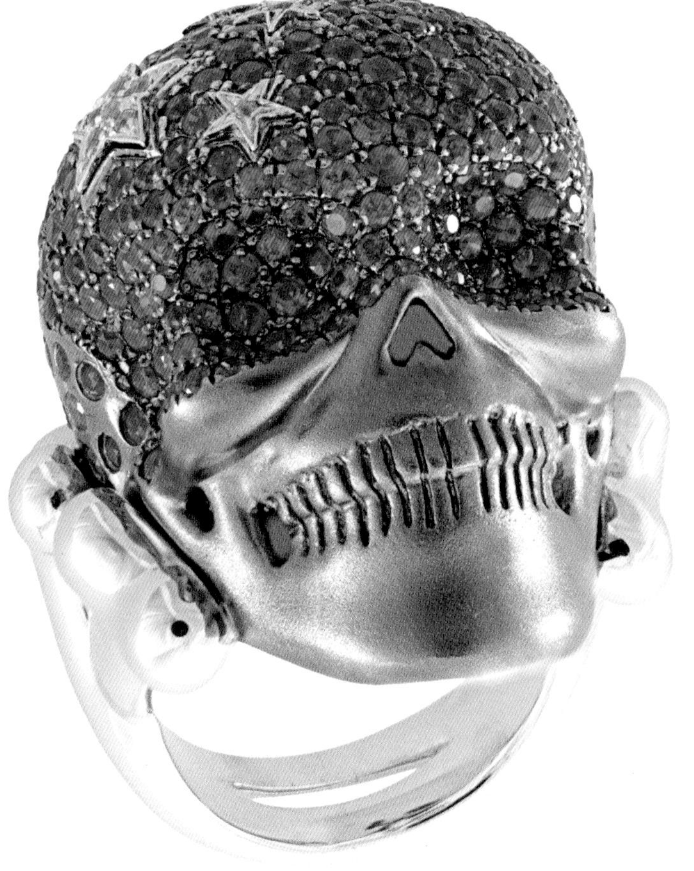

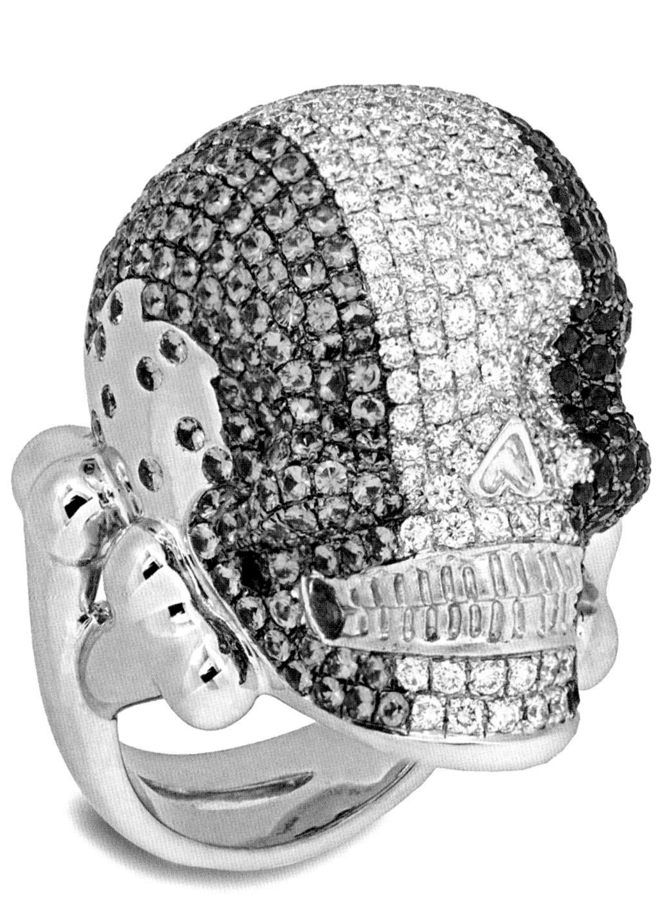

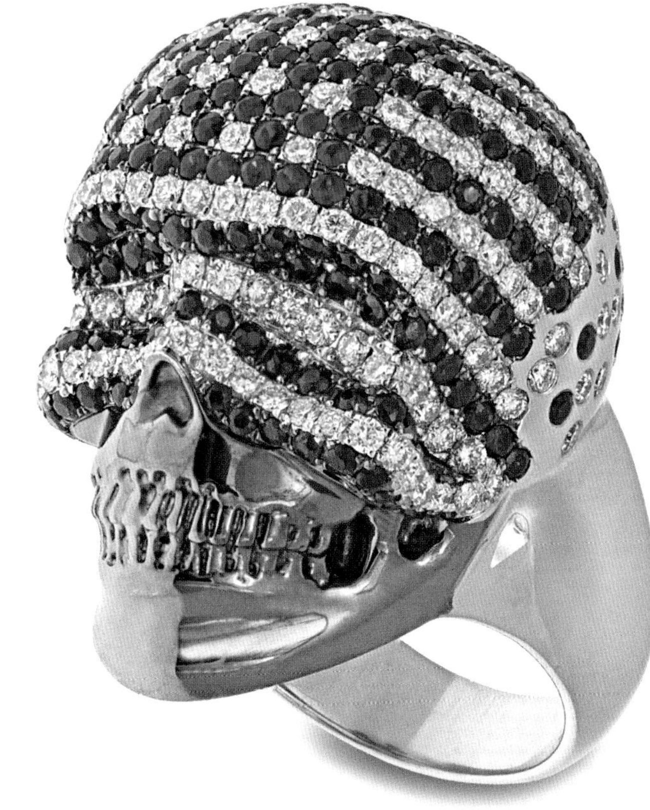

ABOVE LEFT:
ITALIAN TRICOLORE VANITAS RING – TSAVORITE GARNET, RUBY, DIAMOND, WHITE GOLD

ABOVE RIGHT:
STARS & STRIPES VANITAS RING – RUBY, SAPPHIRE, DIAMOND, BLACK RHODIUM-PLATED GOLD, WHITE GOLD

RIGHT:
UNION JACK VANITAS RING – RUBY, SAPPHIRE, DIAMOND, BLACK RHODIUM-PLATED GOLD

OR FETICHE

We know so much about the past two thousand years but little from before then, so we imagine – which is exciting. I love African art which has ancient traditions going back ten thousand years.

OR FETICHE – AFRICA (2006)

ABOVE:
'AFRICAN MASK' RING – LAPIS LAZULI, SAPPHIRE, DIAMOND, GOLD

PREVIOUS SPREAD:
FROM NATURAL WOODS AND ANTIQUE MASKS, LYDIA COURTEILLE CREATES A COLLECTION THAT IS AN HOMAGE TO THE CREATIVITY AND DIVERSITY OF THE AFRICAN CONTINENT
Digital image by Natalie Shau

This collection was inspired first and foremost by a meeting with the great Parisian antiquarian and collector Michel Perinct.

"He excited my curiosity and revealed to me the beauty of African art."

Courteille went on to discover the influences of these tribal arts on the works of the Fauvists, André Derain and Henri Matisse. *Les Demoiselles d'Avignon* by Pablo Picasso and his use of African masks also caught Courteille's eye.

A jewel by Georges Fouquet was also a catalyst for this original collection: Courteille saw it in the Musée des Arts Décoratifs exhibition catalogue, *'Les Fouquet, bijoutiers et joailliers à Paris'*. The jewel by Fouquet was based on a design by André Léveillé (1880-1962) and featured an African mask set with diamond, wood and fine gemstones. Another artist to have influenced her choices in this collection was Jean Lambert-Rucki (1888-1967) friend of Modigliani and Soutine. His sculptures were influenced by African masks and had (according to an essay by François Mathey) similarities with the research executed by other Cubists of the time.

Ebony, scarabs, gemstones and gold come together to create Courteille's African masks, carved in wood and decorated with ancient fertility symbols. For Courteille, the collection is an homage to the creativity and the ideas of the diverse cultures of Africa; she is always fascinated with how works of art can be made from nothing:

"...how a hedgehog can be made from just nails and wood to become a fetish doll bringing good luck."

Like Picasso and Matisse, Courteille spent many hours at the Musée national des Arts d'Afrique et d'Océanie (National Museum of Arts of Africa and Oceania), where she studied the works of art and first encountered 'primitivism'. Later, the Musée du quai Branly in Paris became a favourite haunt, where she continued to learn about tribal works of art. A trip to the Maasai in Kenya and to the Mursi in Ethiopia, helped crystallise Courteille's ideas, and thus began her 'Or Fetiche' collection.

African masks have religious, spiritual and ancestral meanings. They are important in many tribal rituals and initiation ceremonies. Colour associations and the type of wood used, all represent and send a message to the onlooker.

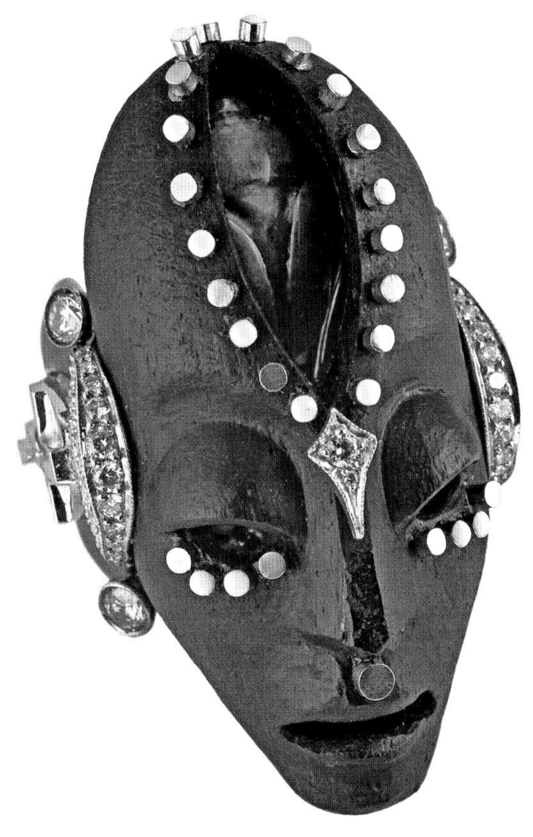

ABOVE LEFT:
'AFRICAN MASK' RING, c.2007 – EBONY, ANCIENT EGYPTIAN CERAMIC SCARAB, BROWN DIAMOND, WHITE GOLD, YELLOW GOLD, ROSE GOLD
Note the mixture of cultures: Lydia Courteille uses an ancient scarab from Egypt with an African mask detail.

ABOVE RIGHT:
'AFRICAN MASK' RING, c.2007 – BLUE AND YELLOW SAPPHIRE, BLACK DIAMOND,BLACK RHODIUM-PLATED GOLD, GOLD

Courteille takes these masks and gives them a new life and meaning, dressing them in gold and gemstones, to create an object as well as a jewel to be valued.

Smooth high oval foreheads and small mouths feature on many of Courteille's masks. They are a symbol of beauty for the Ashanti culture in Ghana. Neck collars (a symbol of wealth), dressed with diamonds and tresses of golden hair decorate these noble features.

Akau'maa, wooden fertility dolls resemble the shape of the Ankh, the ancient Egyptian symbol of life. In Ghana, these dolls are a symbol of youth and fertility. Courteille is interested in the use of fertility dolls and how important they were in the everyday lives of the tribes people; they represent the ancestors and spirits and as such they are used to invoke protection, prosperity and good luck as well as fertility.

Courteille combines colours, enamels and diamonds as well as woods such as ebony, mahogony and lemonwood, with imaginary symbols and antique jewels from other parts of the globe to create juxtapositions and a meeting of cultures. A perfect example is her large pendant with a death mask at its centre, surrounded by tiger's claws, which came from an early 19th-century Chinese jewel.

The jewels were made in Courteille's workshops, where old artisanal techniques helped create a collection that was authentic and iconic. The gold work was all crafted by hand, giving each jewel an imperfect finish, adding to the appeal of each individual piece.

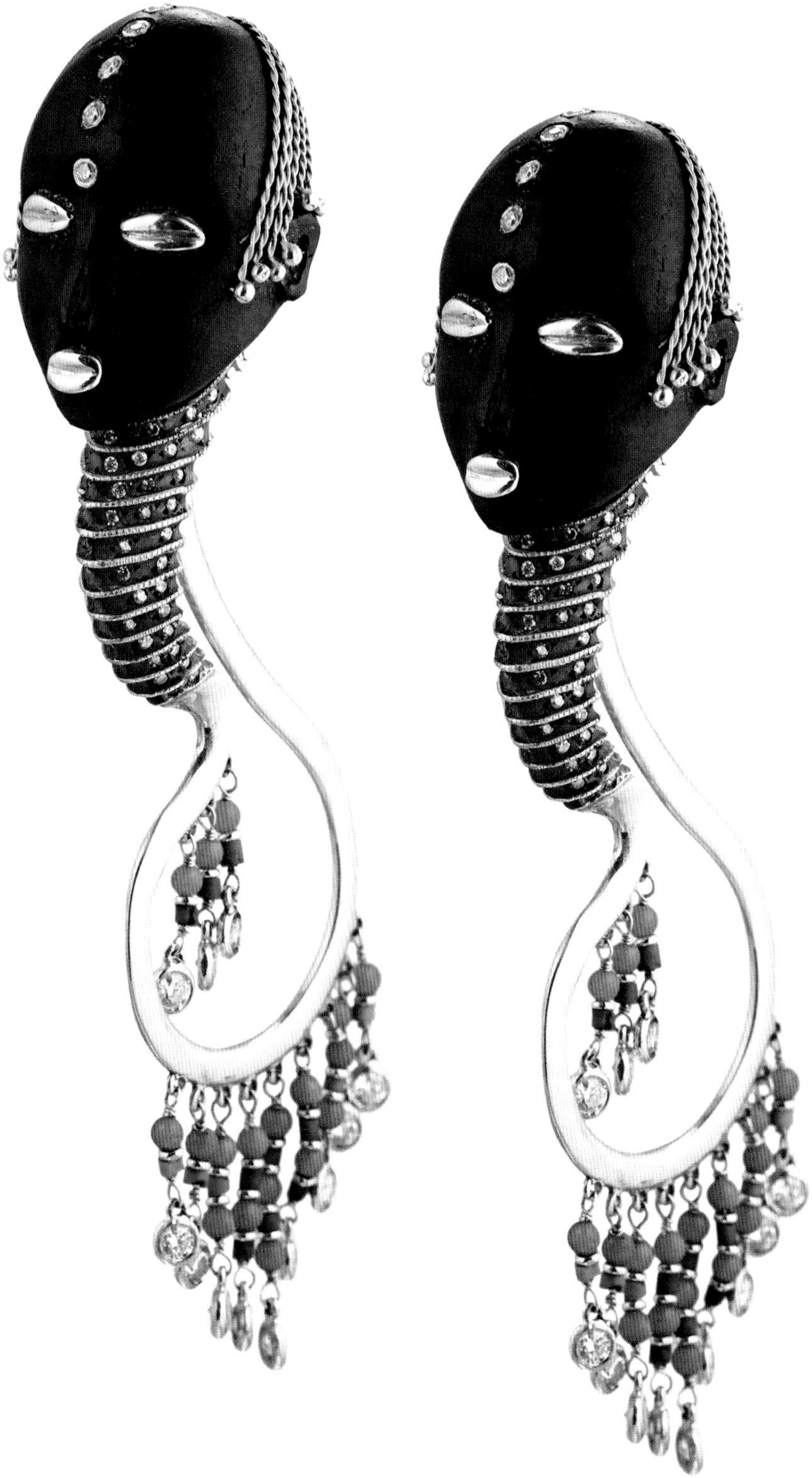

OPPOSITE PAGE:
'OR FETICHE' CUFF – EBONY, BLACK AND CHAMPAGNE-COLOURED DIAMONDS, BLACK RHODIUM-PLATED GOLD, GOLD

ABOVE LEFT:
'ASHANTI WARRIOR' RING – EBONY, DIAMOND, GOLD

RIGHT:
'ASHANTI' EAR PENDANTS – EBONY, CORAL, TURQUOISE, BROWN AND WHITE DIAMOND, GOLD

ABOVE:
'AFRICAN MAASAI' RING – TURQUOISE, ROSE-CUT DIAMOND, BLACK RHODIUM-PLATED GOLD, TEXTURED GOLD

OPPOSITE PAGE:
'OR FETICHE' NECKLACE – ANTIQUE WOODEN MASK, TIGERS' CLAWS, CHAMPAGNE-COLOURED DIAMOND, GOLD

PLATE IX

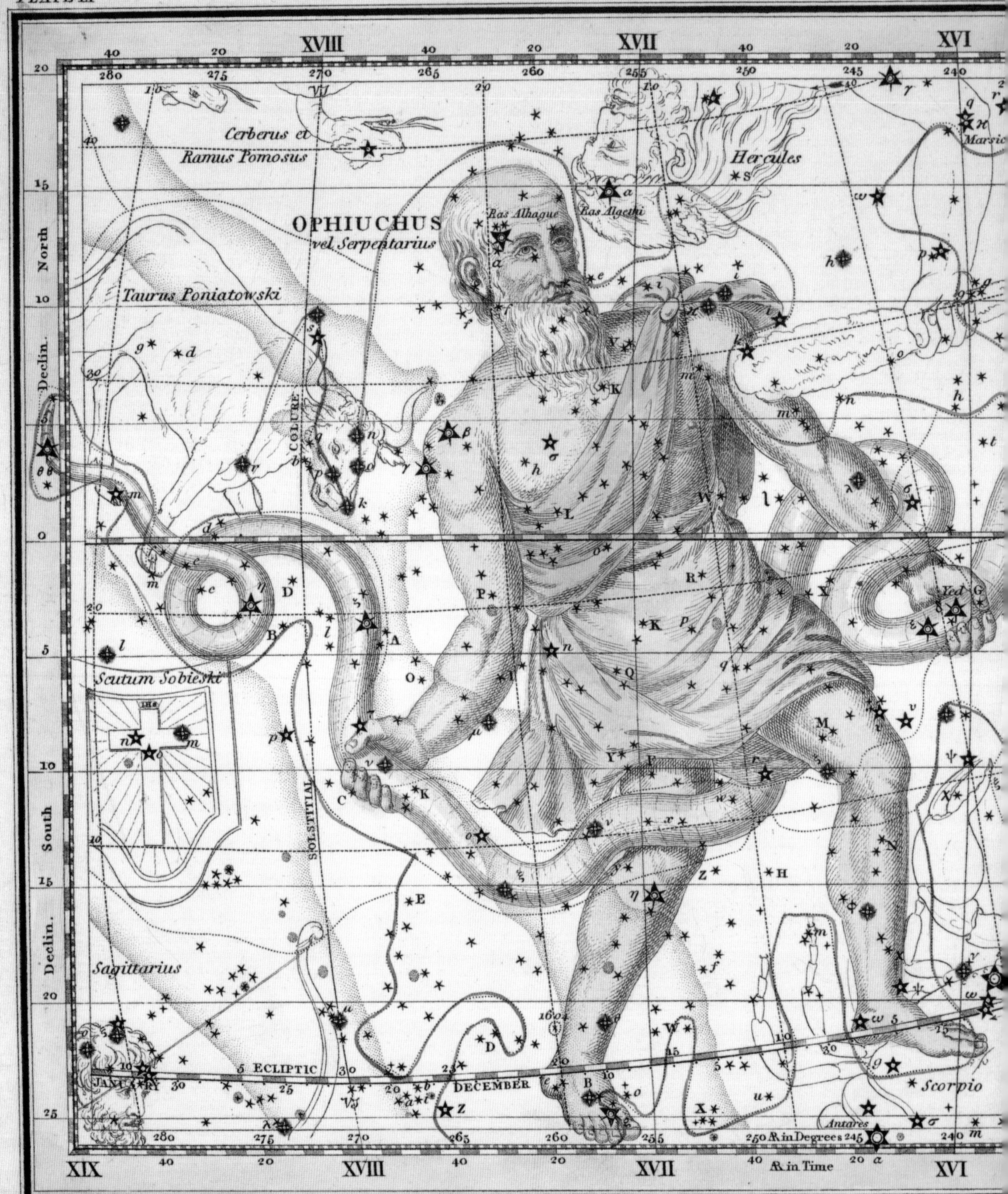
OPHIUCHUS
vel Serpentarius
Hercules
Ras Alhague
Ras Algethi
Cerberus et
Ramus Pomosus
Taurus Poniatowski
Scutum Sobieski
Sagittarius
Scorpio
Antares
Yed
Marsic
COLURE
SOLSTITIAL
ECLIPTIC
JANUARY
DECEMBER
North
Declin.
South
Declin.
XIX
XVIII
XVII
XVI
℞ in Degrees
℞ in Time

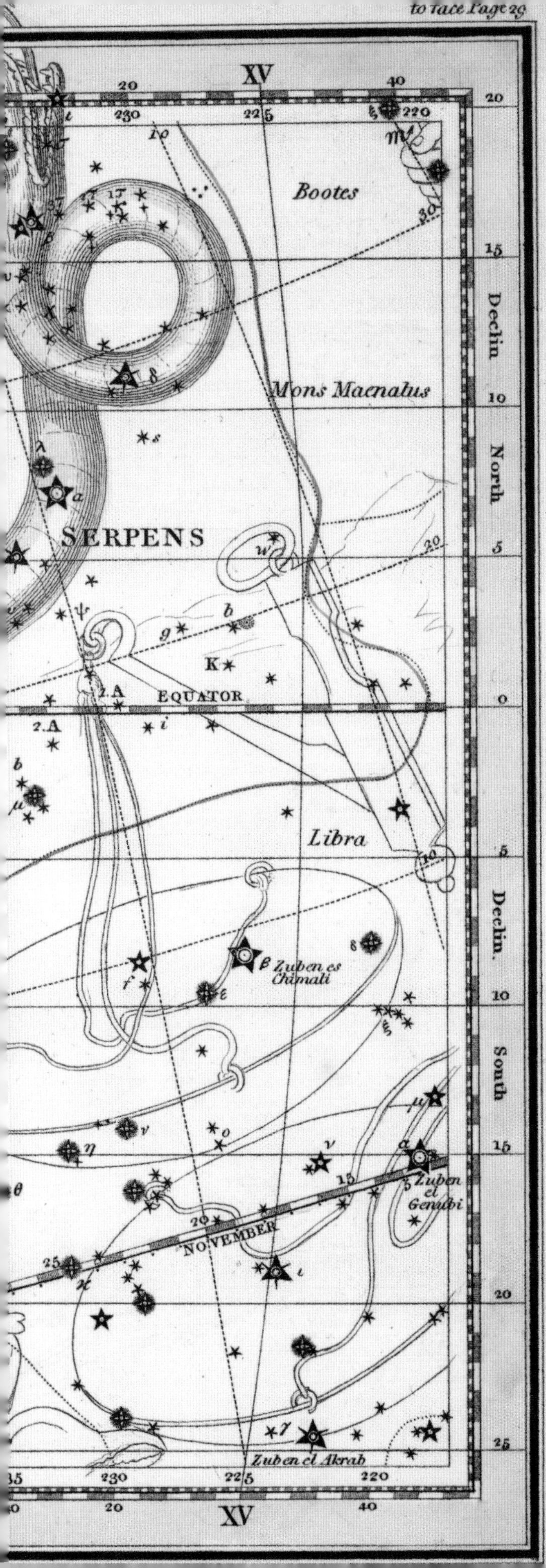

13TH SIGN

13TH SIGN OPHIUCHUS – THE SERPENT BEARER (2006)

Ophiuchus is the serpent bearer. He is the 13th sign in astrology, forgotten, omitted from the zodiac even though the sun passes through his constellation before reaching Sagittarius. He is associated with Asclepius, son of Apollo and is attributed with the qualities of bringing the dead back to life. With a fascination for the *memento mori*, Courteille brings the serpent bearer back to our consciousness after discovering it in ancient Egyptian astrology. The serpent-entwined staff of Asclepius, and more recently the twin-snaked *caduceus*, as symbols of medicine and healing are not lost on Courteille. Courteille invites the wearer to look and to ponder upon the contradictions of life and death.

This collection celebrates the zodiac, but the zodiac with a difference. Illustrator, Armelle Fontaine's thought and skill have enhanced each of Courteille's astrological rings. It is only with careful observation that the symbolic detail is revealed: curling scorpion tails, diamond-studded manes, lion's claws, and bull's, ram's and goat's horns. Each has its own world represented, decorating the borders of large, individual and unusual gemstones. Each ring and set of asymmetric earrings picks up the astrological theme and is elaborated with witticisms.

PREVIOUS SPREAD:
A PAGE FROM ALEXANDER JAMIESON'S *CELESTIAL ATLAS* SHOWING OPHIUCHUS, THE SERPENT BEARER,1822
Courtesy Linda Hall Library of Science, Engineering & Technology

RIGHT:
'PISCES' RING – AMETHYST, TSAVORITE GARNET, RUBY, PINK SAPPHIRE, DIAMOND, BLACK RHODIUM-PLATED GOLD

OPPOSITE PAGE, TOP RIGHT:
'CANCER' RING – RUBELLITE, RUBY, PINK SAPPHIRE, CHAMPAGNE-COLOURED DIAMOND, BLACK RHODIUM-PLATED GOLD, GOLD

OPPOSITE PAGE, LEFT:
'ARIES' RING – BROWN MOONSTONE, SPINEL, RUBY, YELLOW SAPPHIRE, CHAMPAGNE-COLOURED DIAMOND, GOLD

OPPOSITE PAGE, BOTTOM RIGHT:
'ARIES' RING – RHODOCHROSITE, RUBY, BLACK AND WHITE DIAMOND, BLACK ENAMEL, BLACK RHODIUM-PLATED GOLD

OPPOSITE PAGE:
'LEO' EAR PENDANTS – ORANGE AND YELLOW SAPPHIRE, CHRYSOBERYL, BLACK AND WHITE DIAMOND, TSAVORITE GARNET, GOLD

TOP LEFT:
'SCORPION' EAR PENDANTS – RUBELLITE, DIAMOND, BLACK RHODIUM-PLATED GOLD, GOLD

TOP RIGHT:
'CAPRICORN' EAR PENDANTS – ORANGE AND YELLOW SAPPHIRE, FIRE OPAL, EBONY, DIAMOND, GOLD

LEFT:
'PISCES' EAR PENDANTS – AMETHYST, PURPLE SAPPHIRE, GOLD

AMAZONIA

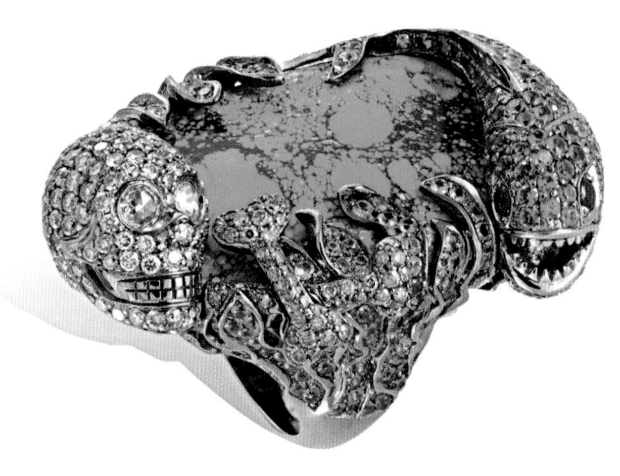

ABOVE:
PIRANHA FISH RING – GREEN TURQUOISE, TSAVORITE GARNET, RUBY, CHAMPAGNE-COLOURED DIAMOND, WHITE GOLD

ABOVE RIGHT:
FROG ON LILY PAD RING – GREEN TURQUOISE, TSAVORITE GARNET, CHAMPAGNE-COLOURED DIAMOND, BLACK DIAMOND, BLACK RHODIUM-PLATED GOLD
Courteille is playing with matte and bright surfaces in this collection.

BELOW:
VINE PENDANT EARRINGS – GREEN TURQUOISE, TSAVORITE GARNET, CHAMPAGNE-COLOURED DIAMOND, WHITE GOLD

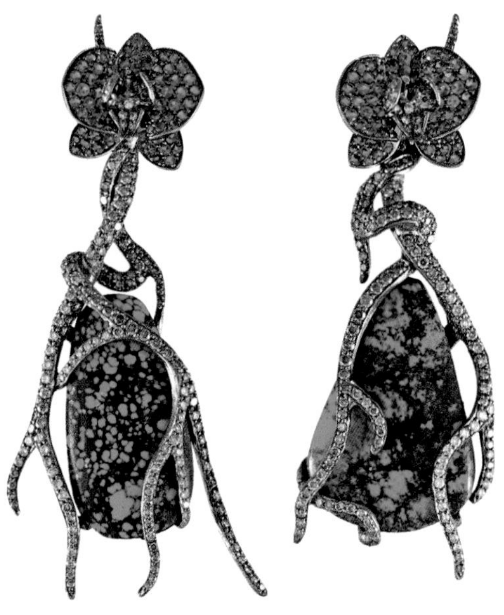

“Green is a colour which brings happiness and people need to breathe.”

AMAZONIA (2012)

The turquoise used in this collection comes from the mines of Gyzylarbat in Turkmanistan beyond the turquoise mountains of Iran and north of the great ancient bronze age civilisation of Merv, near the oasis town of Gonur Depe on the Silk Road. When Courteille first encountered the deep green of this gem she was instantly transported:

“What counted for me the most, was the very bright vivid-green turquoise colour. I felt that this green gave me a source of fresh air; allowing me to breathe. For me it was a beautiful way to resist the polluted urban life – to dream about tropical forests, plants and animals and feel the freshness of pure oxygen.”

She married this feeling with her trip to Brazil in 1997, when she stayed in Amazonia and it was here that she was struck by the intensity of the greens of her surroundings, an image which is forever imprinted in her mind. She thought of old, forgotten Hispanic missionaries and decaying churches disappearing under the weight of lianas, beneath the tropical Amazonian canopy. Her jewels are her interpretation of this world, with bats, beetles, shimmering-skinned amphibians and polished flower petals all competing for a place in a collection furnished with mottled-green turquoise paths and bright surfaces reflecting the humid, moisture-heavy mists of the forest’s undergrowth contrasting with the matte surfaces cutting through the dense jungle.

The variety of hues: the chlorophyll greens and the greens of Madelaine Castaing’s wallpapers, with her singular mix of greens and blues, all played their role in Courteille’s imagination. From these beginnings, the ‘Amazonia’ collection started to take shape.

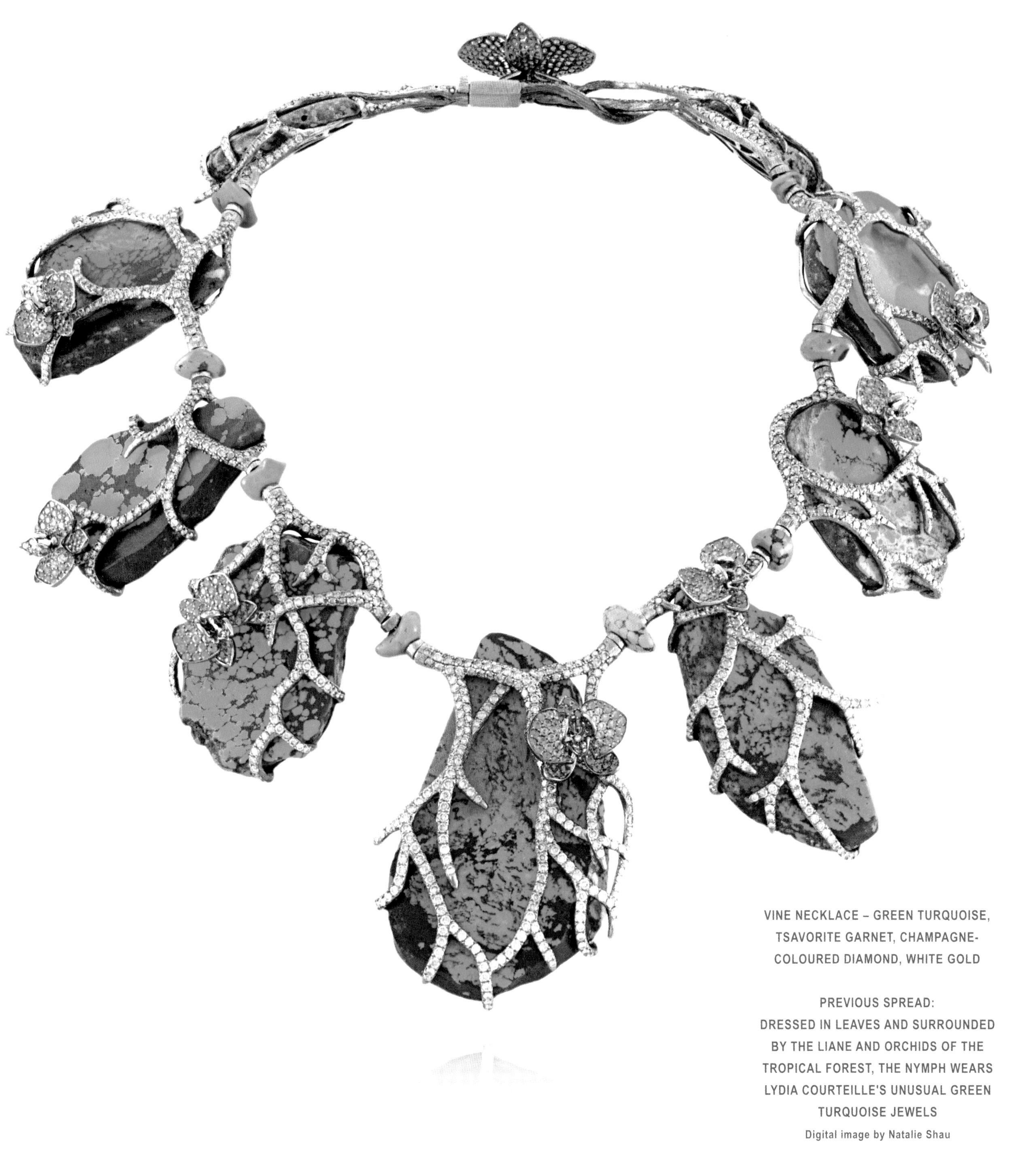

VINE NECKLACE – GREEN TURQUOISE, TSAVORITE GARNET, CHAMPAGNE-COLOURED DIAMOND, WHITE GOLD

PREVIOUS SPREAD:
DRESSED IN LEAVES AND SURROUNDED BY THE LIANE AND ORCHIDS OF THE TROPICAL FOREST, THE NYMPH WEARS LYDIA COURTEILLE'S UNUSUAL GREEN TURQUOISE JEWELS

Digital image by Natalie Shau

RIGHT:
LATIN CROSS RING – GREEN TURQUOISE, TSAVORITE GARNET, BLACK RHODIUM-PLATED GOLD
Lydia Courteille is alluding to the abandoned missionary churches, which have been reclaimed by nature in the rainforest.

BELOW:
PARROT PENDANT EARRINGS – GREEN TURQUOISE, TSAVORITE GARNET, RUBY, CHAMPAGNE-COLOURED DIAMOND, BLACK RHODIUM-PLATED GOLD

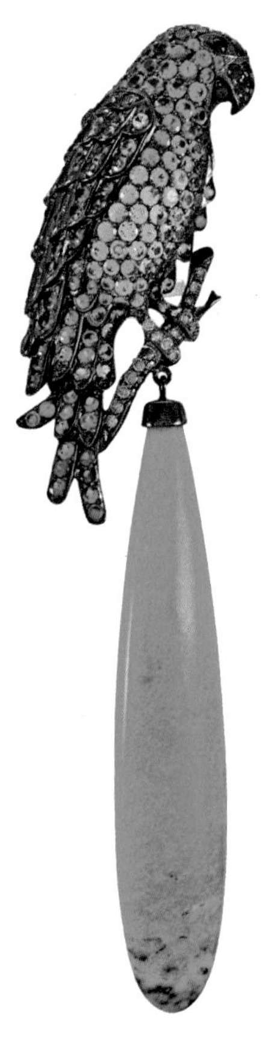

LEFT:
BRACELET – GREEN TURQUOISE, EMERALD, TSAVORITE GARNET, CHAMPAGNE-COLOURED DIAMOND, BLACK RHODIUM-PLATED GOLD

BELOW:
PRIZE-WINNING BRACELET – GREEN TURQUOISE, EMERALD, TSAVORITE GARNET, CHAMPAGNE-COLOURED DIAMOND, BLACK RHODIUM-PLATED GOLD
This bracelet was awarded a prize at the Las Vegas Couture Awards for use of colour in 2012; and was Champion of Champions at the IJDE in 2013

"What counted for me the most, was the very bright vivid-green turquoise colour. I felt that this green gave me a source of fresh air; allowing me to breathe. For me it was a beautiful way to resist the polluted urban life - to dream about tropical forests, plants and animals and feel the freshness of pure oxygen."

ABOVE:
MASK EAR PENDANTS – GREEN TURQUOISE, TSAVORITE GARNET, BLACK RHODIUM-PLATED GOLD
This piece is a link between the 'Amazonia' collection and the'Xochimilco Gardens' collection.

LEFT:
BUTTERFLY DOUBLE FINGER RING – GREEN TURQUOISE, EMERALD, TSAVORITE GARNET, CHAMPAGNE-COLOURED DIAMOND, BLACK RHODIUM-PLATED GOLD

OPPOSITE PAGE:
WINDOW DISPLAY OF 'AMAZONIA' COLLECTION BY HERVÉ SAUVAGE

GARDENS OF XOCHIMILCO

*Mexican fire opal is found on the high Mexican plateaux of Querétaro and Jalisco, which were originally covered by forgotten seas and where ancient volcanoes spewed up silica-rich lava.

Water seeped into the nooks and crevices in that lava mixing with iron oxide. Silica, carried by the water, formed a gel and slowly over millions of years solidified to form opal. Water particles trapped inside the opal create the spectrum effect of colours. Fire opal is now mined from huge canyon-like open-cast mines, traced with high cliff-like walls and winding paths.

OPPOSITE PAGE:
'SERPENT' EAR PENDANTS – FIRE OPAL, BLACK OPAL, RUBY, TSAVORITE GARNET, BLACK RHODIUM-PLATED GOLD

BELOW:
'TURTLE' RING – FIRE OPAL, RUBY, TSAVORITE GARNET, CHAMPAGNE-COLOURED DIAMOND, BLACK RHODIUM-PLATED GOLD, YELLOW GOLD

PREVIOUS SPREAD:
THE MAGNIFICENT PLAYS OF COLOUR TO BE FOUND IN MEXICAN FIRE OPAL ARE USED AS A COMMON THREAD TO BRING TOGETHER THE GARDENS OF XOCHIMILCO AND THE SMALL CREATURES WHO LIVE THERE, WITH THE STRONG CULTURAL BELIEFS OF THE MEXICAN PEOPLE AND THE ANCIENT MESOAMERICAN PYRAMIDS OF TEOTIHUACAN
Digital image by Natalie Shau

GARDENS OF XOCHIMILCO (2010)

The 'Xochimilco' collection was inspired by memories of Courteille's first trip abroad, to Mexico, at the age of just 21. However, it wasn't until 2010 that she started working on this highly original collection, using Mexican fire opals* as her starting point.

It is the magnificent play of colour in the bright orange translucent Mexican opals that earned them their local name, 'Quetzalitzlipyollitli' – stone of the Bird of Paradise – because of the resemblance to these birds' stunning plumage. Remembering how the colourful yellow, orange and red flat-bottomed 'trajineras' (boats) wended their way through the sinuous canals of the famous floating gardens of Xochimilco, Courteille turned to the vivid hues of these transparent and translucent gemstones.

They recall the sun, holidays and moments of joy and wellbeing, *"a plug of vitamin C"*.

Courteille creates multi-layered and colourful stories for each of these pieces by associating them with the folk traditions of Mexico; using the Christian beliefs that swirl about the Santa Muerta and the animist beliefs of the Mayan civilisations, *"a symbol of the resistance to different beliefs"*.

In the astro-architecture of the Mayan civilisation and at the equinoxes of Spring and Autumn, a two-headed snake slowly unfurls its undulating body at the base of the pyramid, in Chichén Itzá. The shadow from the sun creates the feather serpent god – Kukulkan, or 'Quetzalcoatl', as it is named by the Teotihuacan civilisation.

The flora and fauna of Mexico came later, the jewels, each reflecting nature as it is, its beauty and its cruelty provoking thought and taking the wearer on their own private journey.

'FLORAL' NECKLACE – FIRE OPAL, RUBY, TSAVORITE GARNET, MULTI-COLOURED SAPPHIRE, DIAMOND, BLACK RHODIUM-PLATED GOLD, YELLOW GOLD

Note the beetles crawling over the necklace.

ABOVE:
'HUMMING BIRD' EARRINGS – FIRE OPAL, RUBY, YELLOW TOURMALINE, TSAVORITE GARNET, BLACK DIAMOND, BLACK RHODIUM-PLATED GOLD

BELOW:
XOCHIMILCO GARDENS WINDOW DISPLAY BY HERVÉ SAUVAGE

OPPOSITE PAGE:
'SANTA MUERTA' PENDANT – FIRE OPAL, RUBY, TSAVORITE GARNET, GREEN TOURMALINE, MULTI-COLOURED SAPPHIRES, CHAMPAGNE-COLOURED DIAMOND, WHITE DIAMOND, BLACK AND RED TRANSLUCENT ENAMEL, BLACK RHODIUM-PLATED GOLD, WHITE GOLD

> *"Xochimilco was historically the bread basket of the Xochomilco and Aztec populations of pre-Hispanic times."*

BELOW:
SCORPION RING – FIRE OPAL, YELLOW AND ORANGE SAPPHIRES, TSAVORITE GARNET, BLACK DIAMOND, BLACK RHODIUM-PLATED GOLD

OPPOSITE PAGE:
'SALAMANDER AND INSECT' BROOCH – FIRE OPAL, MULTI-COLOURED SAPPHIRE, TSAVORITE GARNET, SPESSARTITE GARNET, CHAMPAGNE-COLOURED DIAMOND, WHITE DIAMOND, BLACK RHODIUM-PLATED GOLD, YELLOW GOLD

> *"The Feather serpent - long bodied brooch with ornate tail decorated in fire. It has already witnessed the human sacrifices made in its name."*

ABOVE:
'QUETZALCOATL' RING – FIRE OPAL, RUBY, MULTI-COLOURED SAPPHIRE, DIAMOND, BLACK RHODIUM-PLATED GOLD

OPPOSITE PAGE:
'FEATHER SERPENT' BROOCH – FIRE OPAL, RUBY, MULTI-COLOURED SAPPHIRE, DIAMOND, BLACK RHODIUM-PLATED GOLD

HOMAGE TO SURREALISM

HOMAGE TO SURREALISM (2011)

Surrealism grasped hold of Courteille's imagination when she discovered a book introducing her to the world of Salvador Dalí (published by Draeger in 1968). From this dawning interest, she discovered Louise Bourgeois' impressive spider sculptures. Marrying their worlds with that of the great 15th-century artist, Hieronymus Bosch, Courteille conceived her 'Homage to Surrealism' collection.

Together, the paintings *Geopoliticus child watching the Birth of the New Man,* by Salvador Dalí,*The Garden of Earthly Delights* by Bosch and *Concert in the Egg,* an old copy of a lost work by Bosch, all served as inspiration for a Skeleton and Egg ring; a reminder that right from birth, only the end awaits.

Courteille's lobster earrings are a nod to both Dalí's lobster telephone and the Schiaparelli lobster dress worn by Wallis Simpson in Cecil Beaton's photograph for *Vogue* just before her marriage to the Duke of Windsor.

Janine Janet sculptures lend their form to earrings – part man and part vegetation, as 'Adam and Eve', as well as to coral branches transformed into living brooches.

Alongside those of Salvador Dalí, paintings by great Surrealist artists, such as René Magritte and Max Ernst, have taken Courteille on other journeys, inspiring many of her dream-like jewels; elements from René Magritte's distinctive *Shéhérazade* can be seen in her Harem Ring.

ABOVE:
LOBSTER EARRINGS – FIRE OPAL, ORANGE SAPPHIRE, BLACK DIAMOND, YELLOW GOLD

RIGHT:
LOUISE BOURGEOIS' SPIDER SCULPTURE, MAMAN (MOTHER), 1999, INSTALLED OUTSIDE TATE MODERN, LONDON IN 2007

OPPOSITE PAGE:
SPIDER BROOCH – MOONSTONE, SAPPHIRE, TSAVORITE GARNET, WHITE GOLD
Inspired by Louise Bourgeois' sculpture, Mother

PREVIOUS SPREAD:
THE VIOLET-EYED BEAUTY MERGES WITH THE CLOUDS AND THE TRANQUIL WATERS; HER JEWELS ARE INSPIRED BY DALI, MATISSE, AND FROM EARLIER YEARS – ARCIMBOLDO AND HIERONYMUS BOSCH
Digital image by Natalie Shau

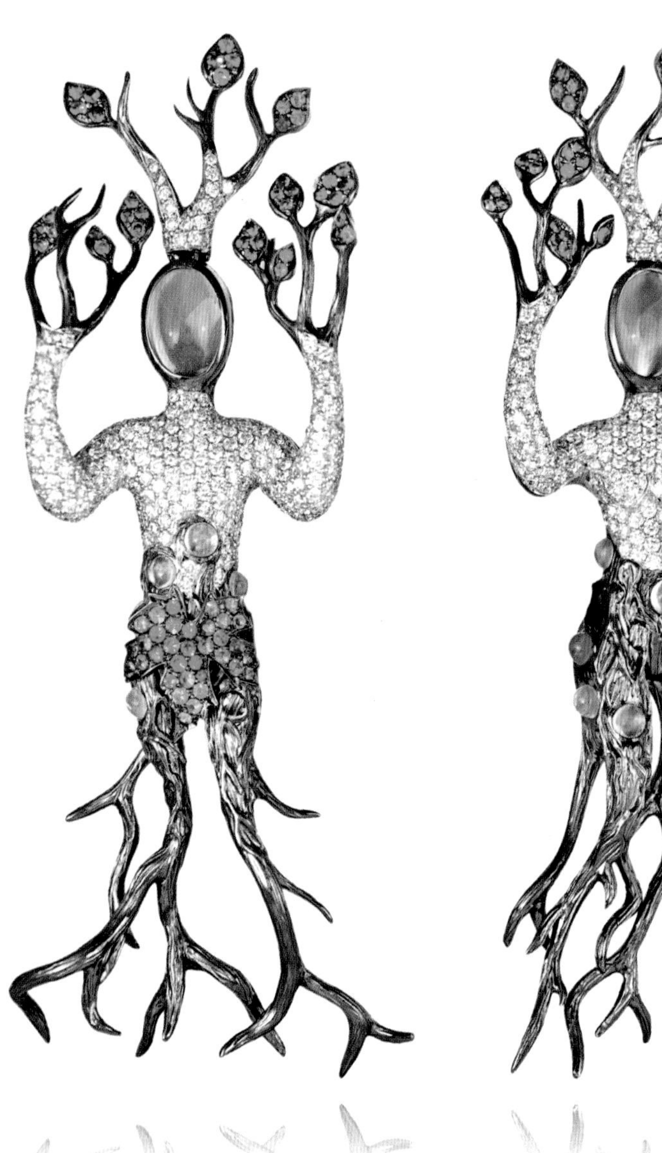

ABOVE LEFT:
ADAM AND EVE EARRINGS – MOONSTONE, GREEN GARNET, SAPPHIRE, DIAMOND, WHITE GOLD
Inspired by Bosch's painting, *The Garden of Earthly Delights* and the tree men that Bosch depicts in the scenes of hell, as well as by the sculptures by Janine Janet.

ABOVE RIGHT:
LYDIA COURTEILLE'S NOTEBOOK OPENED ON A PAGE THAT SHOWS THE PROGRESSION OF HER IDEAS FOR THE HAREM RING, WHICH WAS INSPIRED BY RENÉ MAGRITTE'S *SHÉHÉRAZADE*.

RIGHT:
SHÉHÉRAZADE HAREM RING – BLACK AND WHITE DIAMOND, RED ENAMEL, BLACK RHODIUM-PLATED GOLD

ABOVE LEFT:
DETAIL OF AN EGG FROM *THE GARDEN OF EARTHLY DELIGHTS* BY HIERONYMUS BOSCH
Photograph © Museo Nacional del Prado, Dist. RMN-GP / Image du Prado

ABOVE RIGHT:
GEOPOLITICUS CHILD WATCHING THE BIRTH OF THE NEW MAN 1943, OIL ON CANVAS
© Salvador Dali, Fundació Gala-Salvador Dali, DACS, 2016
Collection of the Salvador Dali Museum Inc., St Petersburg, FL (USA) 2016
© 2016 Salvador Dali Museum, Inc.

RIGHT:
MEMENTO MORI AND EGG RING – CHAMPAGNE-COLOURED DIAMOND, ENAMEL, BLACK RHODIUM-PLATED GOLD

TOP LEFT:
A PAIR OF 'WATCHING EYE' EARRINGS - BLACK AND WHITE DIAMOND, TRANSLUCENT ENAMEL, YELLOW SAPPHIRE, BLACK RHODIUM-PLATED GOLD

TOP RIGHT:
GOUACHE OF ARCIMBOLDO RING
Gouache by Christian Obry

RIGHT:
ARCIMBOLDO RING, c.2007 – GREEN GARNET, YELLOW GOLD
Inspired by the works by Giuseppe Arcimboldo (1527 - 1593).

OPPOSITE PAGE:
MEMENTO MORI STEPPING THROUGH A MIRROR PENDANT – BLACK DIAMOND, BLACK RHODIUM-PLATED GOLD, YELLOW GOLD
The memento mori is looking back on his past and moves between the past, present and the future.

VENDANGE
TARDIVE

ABOVE:
EAR PENDANTS – AMETHYST, TSAVORITE GARNET, PURPLE AND BLUE SAPPHIRE, ENAMEL, CHAMPAGNE-COLOURED DIAMOND, BLACK RHODIUM-PLATED GOLD

PREVIOUS SPREAD:
TAKING HER CUE FROM THE *RAINBOW PORTRAIT* OF QUEEN ELIZABETH I, THE SIREN FINDS HERSELF LURED INTO A FIELD THE COLOUR OF RICH DARK WINE. THE EYES – ALL KNOWING – ARE WATCHING AND WARNING, WHILE THE THUNDER CLOUDS APPROACH
Digital image by Natalie Shau

VENDANGE TARDIVE (2013)

Autumn has come, dark storm clouds gather in the distance, the eyes of the poppies wait for the harvesting of the fruit, in rows of deep purples and greens. The grapes hang heavy from their branches, awaiting harvest...

An extension to 'Homage to Surrealism', this collection brings us home, to Courteille's France. The senses take over: Courteille takes her inspiration from the sweet *'vin de paille'* of the Jura region, which is made using dried grapes; it is a style of wine that has been savoured since antiquity.

Inspired by Dalí's 'Grapes of Immortality' brooch, on which the over-ripe grapes are disguised as vanities, Courteille uses the deep purples of amethysts and the greens of tsavorite garnets against the black background of rhodium-plated gold. The vanities peer from beneath the leaves, dressed in spider webs of champagne diamonds and drops of pearls, wrapped in cloaks of bats' wings.

CUFF – AMETHYST, TSAVORITE GARNET, PURPLE AND BLUE SAPPHIRE, ENAMEL, CHAMPAGNE-COLOURED DIAMOND, TEXTURED BLACK RHODIUM-PLATED GOLD

> *"The portrait states in the painting 'NON SINE SOLE IRIS' – no rainbow without sun."*

ABOVE:
VANITAS EAR PENDANTS – AMETHYST, TSAVORITE GARNET, PURPLE AND BLUE SAPPHIRE, ENAMEL, CHAMPAGNE-COLOURED DIAMOND, PEARLS, BLACK RHODIUM-PLATED GOLD

ABOVE RIGHT:
VANITAS EAR PENDANTS – AMETHYST, TSAVORITE GARNET, PURPLE AND BLUE SAPPHIRE, ENAMELLED BAT WINGS, BLACK RHODIUM-PLATED GOLD

OPPOSITE:
***THE RAINBOW PORTRAIT OF ELIZABETH I*, ATTRIBUTED VARIOUSLY TO ISAAC OLIVER OR MARCUS GHEERAERTS THE YOUNGER, c.1600-1602**

By kind permission of the Marquess of Salisbury, Hatfield House

Lydia Courteille was very taken by this allegorical portrait of Elizabeth I, which shows her as a young woman even though it was in fact painted towards the end of her life. Note the serpent and the famous 'all knowing eyes and ears' embroidered on her dress.

NON SINE SOLE
IRIS.

LOST
AT
SEA

ABYSSE

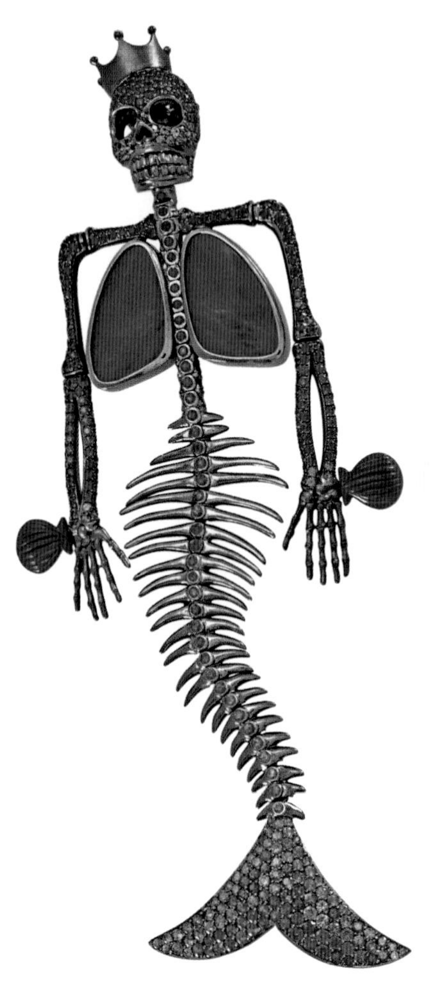

ABYSSE – DEEP SEA (c.2013)

Luc Besson's cinematic feast *Le Grand Bleu* and the classic novel *Twenty Thousand Leagues under the Sea* by Jules Vernes conjure up travels to deep unknown destinations, from the lost city of Atlantis to the underwater forests of the fictional Island of Crespo on the ocean floor. Inspired by the stunning iridescent blues and greens of Australian boulder opals and the matte rust, brown and ochre colours that contrast with this opalescence, Courteille sees an underwater ambience of another world, of rocks and hidden grottoes.This is her imaginary world, her pareidolia, a 'landscape' of giant colourful coral reefs throwing shadows on the seabed, where giant octopus and huge cuttlefish roam and where Courteille's creatures of make-believe, come together.

"I love to look for shapes in the boulder opals, in the same way that as a child one tried to find animals in the clouds."

Phantasmagorical winged sea-horses live side-by-side with aquatic siren vanities. Creatures on the seabed are dressed in pink, blue and purple sapphires, contrasting and enhancing the deep colours from the boulder opals, which are the real stars of this collection.

> *"The gems look like a small aquarium or a photograph of the deep sea. There is an enigmatic mood in these stones, magical and mysterious like the legend of Atlantis."*

That plankton has a similar chemical structure to opal has not been lost on Courteille, who plays with the theme of the sea and the plankton that lives there, using opal as the bridge between the sea and her magical world.

One of the brooches from this collection was a winner at the AGTA 2014 awards, acclaimed for her attention to detail and the exquisite way that she picked out the colours of the opal using a detailed pavé setting in blue and pink sapphires. Courteille credits the workshop that helped create this prize-winning brooch.

ABOVE LEFT:
SEA MER-SKELETON PENDANT – BOULDER OPAL, PURPLE AND BLUE SAPPHIRE, BLUE ENAMEL, BLACK RHODIUM-PLATED GOLD

ABOVE CENTRE:
A CONSTELLATION OF STARFISH RING – SAPPHIRE (PURPLE, YELLOW, ORANGE AND PINK), TSAVORITE GARNET, DIAMOND, BLACK RHODIUM-PLATED GOLD

ABOVE RIGHT:
OCTOPUS BROOCH – SAPPHIRE (PURPLE, YELLOW, PINK AND BLUE), AMETHYST, SPINEL, BLACK RHODIUM-PLATED GOLD

PREVIOUS SPREAD:
SIREN OF THE DEEP, WEARING A DIADEM OF BLUE SAPPHIRE STARFISH SURROUNDED BY LYDIA COURTEILLE'S IMAGINARY CREATURES
Digital image by Natalie Shau

SEAHORSE RING c.2012 – BOULDER OPAL, SAPPHIRE (PURPLE, PINK AND BLUE), TSAVORITE GARNET, DIAMOND, BLACK RHODIUM-PLATED GOLD

Note how the sapphires pick up and emphasise the colours in the Boulder opal.
This was the prize-winning jewel for the AGTA Awards for Colour, 2014

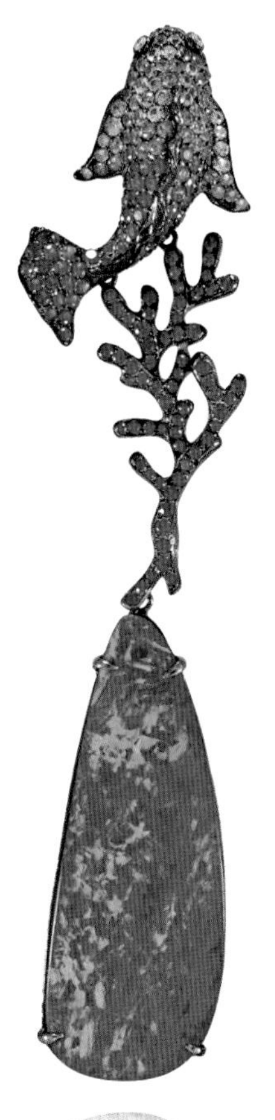

ABOVE:
ABYSSE EAR PENDANTS – BOULDER OPAL, PURPLE AND BLUE SAPPHIRE, TSAVORITE GARNET, BLACK RHODIUM-PLATED GOLD, WHITE GOLD

RIGHT:
OCTOPUS PENDANT – BOULDER OPAL, PURPLE AND BLUE SAPPHIRE, TSAVORITE GARNET, DIAMOND, BLACK RHODIUM-PLATED GOLD

OPPOSITE PAGE:
CUTTLEFISH RING – WHITE OPAL, BLUE SAPPHIRE, DIAMOND, BLACK RHODIUM-PLATED GOLD, WHITE GOLD

GYPSET – THE HIPPY HERITAGE

Courteille's wonderful whimsical 'Gypset' collection has its origin in the phrase coined by the journalist Julia Chaplin, who used it to describe two very different worlds – the bringing together of the hip with the chic, rich and cultured, two worlds which in theory have little in common. The rich and beautiful, who jet about the world to intimate, elitist haunts and the nomadic bohemian lifestyle of artists and gypsies. Courteille uses the old artisanal techniques of enamelling from around the world and marries them with the colourful '70s hippy fashions of the dedicated gypset girl adding bright gemstone drops that catch the light as they move.

RIGHT:
'GYPSET'' EAR PENDANT, OWL WITH OUTSPREAD WINGS, c.2014 – BLUE, YELLOW AND PINK SAPPHIRE, TOPAZ, TSAVORITE GARNET, RUBY, ENAMEL, BLACK RHODIUM-PLATED GOLD, YELLOW GOLD

FAR RIGHT:
'GYPSET' EAR PENDANT, CRAB WITH STARFISH AND SHELLS, c.2014 – RUBY, SAPPHIRE (ORANGE, YELLOW, BLUE, PURPLE AND PINK), ENAMEL, BLACK RHODIUM-PLATED GOLD, YELLOW GOLD

OPPOSITE PAGE:
WANDERLUST AND CULTURE MIX TOGETHER TO BRING HIPPY TO CHIC AND CHIC TO HIPPY. LYDIA COURTEILLE'S JEWELLED KITES ARE THE TRAVELLER'S DRESS CODE
Digital image by Natalie Shau

LAPIN ROSE

BELOW LEFT:
PINK BUNNY RING: RUBELLITE, PINK SAPPHIRE, CHAMPAGNE-COLOURED DIAMOND, BLACK DIAMOND, ROSE GOLD

BELOW RIGHT:
PINK BUNNY PENDANT EARRINGS – RUBELLITE DROPS, PINK SAPPHIRE, BLACK AND WHITE DIAMONDS, ROSE GOLD

OPPOSITE PAGE:
PINK BUNNY BRACELET – AMETHYST, PINK SAPPHIRE, BLACK AND WHITE DIAMONDS, ROSE TEXTURED GOLD, GOLD

PREVIOUS SPREAD:
RABBITS WITH PINK EYES, RABBIT-SHAPED CLOUDS AND PLAYBOY REFERENCES ARE THE BACKGROUND TO LYDIA COURTEILLE'S ORIGINAL USE OF DEEP PINK TOURMALINE AND RUBELLITE GEMSTONES
Digital image by Natalie Shau

LAPIN ROSE – PINK BUNNY (2012)

Hot on the heels of her 'Homage to Surrealism' collection, Courteille produced the amusing 'Pink Bunny' collection. At her home in Provence, a large chicken coop with several small wooden hutches stood abandoned, a neighbour suggested that she put two pairs of rabbits in the run and lo and behold... six months later...there were 24 little bunnies!

Courteille uses large pink tourmalines or amethysts as the focal point of this collection, setting them within a multitude of hopping and skipping rabbits, pavé-set with pink sapphires, rubies and diamonds. They are a witty statement, a reminder of *Playboy* magazine, and the reality of nature!

“When I went into the chicken run there were baby rabbits jumping all over and that is when I thought about creating a collection of rabbits with attitude. When one thinks ‘bunny, one also thinks Playboy ...I also happened to have some lovely pink tourmaline and hey presto, the pink bunny collection!”

ANIMAL

> *All animals are equal, but some animals are more equal than others.*
> *Animal Farm, George Orwell*

ABOVE:
TURKEY RING – TOPAZ, PINK AND BLUE SAPPHIRE, AMETHYST, BLACK AND WHITE DIAMONDS, BLACK RHODIUM-PLATED GOLD, GOLD

PREVIOUS SPREAD:
OPULENCE AND A CERTAIN FORM OF EQUALITY COME TOGETHER IN THE FORM OF GEORGE ORWELL'S *ANIMAL FARM* AND THE EXCESSES OF THE CHATEAU DE VERSAILLES. MARIE ANTOINETTE IS SHOWN SURROUNDED BY LYDIA COURTEILLE'S CROWNED ANIMALS, WHILST THE STORM CLOUDS GATHER IN THE BACKGROUND, WARNING OF THE TEMPESTUOUS TIMES OF THE FRENCH REVOLUTION TO COME
Digital image by Natalie Shau

ANIMAL FARM – A COLLECTION OF CONTRADICTIONS (2013)

George Orwell's *Animal Farm* is the starting point for Courteille's collection, designed by Armelle Fontaine. The farm is populated with pigs, cows, donkeys, hens, mice and horses just as in the original dystopian novella, which satirises Stalin's Soviet Union.

Each creature in Courteille's 'Animal Farm' wears a jewelled crown in honour of Marie Antoinette's farm at the Chateau of Versailles. Duality is at play in this collection: Monarchy versus Communism.

The collection is provocative and ironic and demands a reaction. Ear pendants have been imagined using the animals' ears – ear to ear – with matching touches of colour and gemstones found in the jewelled rings.

TURKEY EAR PENDANTS – AMETHYST, SEED PEARL, SAPPHIRE, BLACK AND WHITE DIAMONDS, BLACK RHODIUM-PLATED GOLD, GOLD

RIGHT:
DUCK EAR PENDANTS – PEARL, WHITE TOPAZ, ONYX, BLACK ENAMEL, WHITE DIAMOND, GOLD

BELOW LEFT:
DONKEY RING – CHAMPAGNE-COLOURED DIAMONDS, BLACK AND WHITE DIAMONDS, BLACK RHODIUM PLATED GOLD

BELOW RIGHT:
PIG RING – PINK SAPPHIRE, TSAVORITE GARNET, CHAMPAGNE-COLOURED DIAMOND, YELLOW DIAMOND, ROSE GOLD

OPPOSITE PAGE:
MARIE ANTOINETTE BY JEAN-BAPTISTE GAUTIER DAGOTY, 1775

Photograph © REX/Shutterstock

SCARLET EMPRESS

“ *A collection where extremes meet.* ”

MARLENE DIETRICH AND JOHN LODGE IN A STILL FROM JOSEF VON STERNBERG'S 1934 FILM, *THE SCARLET EMPRESS*

SCARLET EMPRESS (2014)

Courteille has always been intrigued by the roles of great women and their contribution to history; Catherine the Great, for example, who married Tzar Peter III and took control of Russia in a coup d'état in 1762.

Courteille was inspired by Catherine the Great's story and the controversial 1934 film, *The Scarlet Empress*, directed by Josef von Sternberg and starring Marlene Dietrich. Sternberg depicted Catherine as a sensual, obsessed woman collecting erotic paraphernalia, as cruel as the country that she ruled. The film was condemned by the Catholic Legion of Decency as being 'morally objectionable'.

Courteille creates her 'plays on words' and uses history and symbolism to create her special duality. When she visited Russia, she was in awe of the splendour of the Kremlin and fascinated by the contradictions of the Soviet Union. Had they not killed their Tsar? Yet they preserved the opulence of the 18th century, its jewelled crowns and Catherine the Great's silver robe. She brings together these threads to create this subversive collection.

Deliberately provocative, Courteille uses typical 18th-century jewellery designs and silhouettes to recall the romance and femininity of a bygone age. She uses figurative witticisms tying the 20th-century Soviet period (represented in red and the Soviet Union's emblems of the hammer and the sickle) to the past, to the 18th century, with its candlelit balls and politics of another age – feathers and masks, mixed with orthodox crosses, and the symbol of Russia's sovereignty, the Imperial double eagle.

Like a Russian doll, her jewels have layer upon layer of meaning, the red of revolution and Communism, the red of the Soviet flag, the red blood spilled by the workers fighting for freedom from serfdom...but red also represents the cruelty of the 18th century; in the French language, 'Alizarine' red, rhymes with *tzarine;* and in Russian, the word for 'red' (красный) is associated with the Russian word for 'beautiful' (красивый). Red is also the colour of a dye used in micro-biology, a hint to Courteille's past life as a biochemist.

LEFT:
HEART RING – RUBELLITE, RED ENAMEL, TEXTURED WHITE GOLD, YELLOW GOLD
The ring symbolises the cruelty of the regime of Catherine the Great.

PREVIOUS SPREAD:
LYDIA COURTEILLE MIXES THE CRUELTY OF CATHERINE THE GREAT'S 18TH-CENTURY RUSSIA WITH THE SYMBOLS OF THE 20TH-CENTURY SOVIET UNION TO CREATE A TOTALLY FEMININE COLLECTION THAT TAKES ITS FORMS FROM 18TH-CENTURY ANTIQUE JEWELLERY. DRESSED IN SPLENDOUR, THE DARK-HAIRED BEAUTY STANDS BEFORE A BACKDROP OF RUSSIAN ORTHODOX FRESCOS. THE SYMBOLS OF THE DOUBLE-HEADED EAGLE, THE ORTHODOX CROSS AND THE COLOUR RED ARE ALL PRESENT
Digital image by Natalie Shau

“Russia was a country which had the most beautiful women!”

CHOKER – RUBELLITE, RUBY, RED SPINEL, RED RHODIUM-PLATED GOLD

Note how Courteille incorporates the Orthodox mitre – a reference to the Russian Orthodox church – and frost crystals, which make a reference to the famous ice jewels of Fabergé from the early 20th century. The central rubellite drop is carved on the reverse with an erotic image of two lovers.

“It’s never too red!”

OPPOSITE PAGE:

HAMMER AND SICKLE/DOUBLE-HEADED EAGLE BRACELET – RUBELLITE, RUBY, RED RHODIUM-PLATED GOLD

Note that this bracelet very effectively shows Lydia Courteille's duality, which is at play in many different ways: the Hammer and Sickle and the colour red represent the Soviet Union, whilst the double-headed eagle and the Russian Orthodox crowns represent the time of Catherine the Great; red also represents the suffering and cruelty of her epoch.

ABOVE LEFT:

ARMOUR BIKER RING – RUBY RUBELITE RED RHODIUM-PLATED GOLD

ABOVE RIGHT:

FEATHER AND MASK EARRINGS, c.2008 – RUBELLITE, RUBY, RED RHODIUM-PLATED GOLD

One of Courteille's popular designs, which finds its way into many of her collections – she calls them her transitional jewels.

LEFT:

OSTRICH FEATHER AND FAN PENDANT EARRINGS – RUBELLITE, RUBY, RED RHODIUM-PLATED GOLD

THE RAINBOW WARRIOR

THE RAINBOW WARRIOR (2014)

Native American tribes all have different interpretations on the significance of a rainbow: for the Navajo it means the path of the holy spirits (Yei) and for the Huron it is the bridge to the sky world.

The story that inspired Lydia Courteille, was a prophesy that had been passed down orally, from generation to generation, in the Cree and Hopi tribes. It tells of a time when the creations of the Great Spirit will be destroyed by the greed of the white man and how the warriors of the rainbow, from every tribe and colour, would gather together to save those designs by re-teaching how to live in the 'Way of the Great Spirit'. *The Rainbow Warrior* is a tale that was published as a book in 1962 and there is much debate about its real origins.

Courteille uses red, black, white and yellow enamels for the feathers in her jewels to represent the four peoples called upon by the Great Spirit, as told in these Hopi and Cree traditions. Rainbow colours appear in the jewels of this collection, feathers on their own or paired with peacock feathers have a special meaning – they are prayers, and symbolise creativity and honour.

As well as the creatures of native American myth and legend, feathers, arrows and the four elements are all present as emblems and symbols. Fine stones are decorated with lightning bolts representing swiftness; turtles are present, bringing long life and protection, they are also a symbol of strength and fertility; whilst the lonely butterfly and frog signify renewal, fertility and the coming of spring; the thunderbird is the sacred bearer of endless happiness.

ABOVE LEFT:
EAGLE EAR PENDANT – CHRYSOCOLLA, TURQUOISE, MULTI-COLOURED SAPPHIRE, TSAVORITE GARNET, BROWN AND WHITE ENAMEL, BROWN RHODIUM-PLATED GOLD

ABOVE RIGHT:
EAR PENDANTS – TURQUOISE, EMERALD, YELLOW SAPPHIRE, RUBY BEADS, DIAMOND, ENAMEL (RED, YELLOW, WHITE AND BLACK), BROWN RHODIUM-PLATED GOLD, YELLOW GOLD

Turquoise and layered chrysocolla have other meanings, which have not been lost on Courteille: chrysocolla is the stone of peace and of teaching, for easing communication, it is believed to be a stone of feminine energy, it is the stone of wise women; turquoise is one of the four materials symbolising the road to life in the Hopi, Pueblo and Zuni traditions (the others are coral, jet and abalone).

For this collection, Courteille has brought together other unusual gemstones, such as sunstone and brown moonstone (this is Hanwi – Night Sun – the Sioux Moon Goddess, who protects people from harm during the night time) into her jewels and married them to rainbow colours set with a myriad of sapphire and garnet hues.

ABOVE:
MOCCASIN RING – TURQUOISE, RUBY, BLUE SAPPHIRE, ZIRCON, RUST-COLOURED ENAMEL, BROWN RHODIUM-PLATED GOLD, YELLOW GOLD

LEFT:
THUNDERCLOUD EAGLE EAR PENDANTS – TURQUOISE, YELLOW SAPPHIRE, COGNAC-COLOURED DIAMOND, BLACK AND WHITE DIAMOND, BROWN RHODIUM-PLATED GOLD, YELLOW GOLD

PREVIOUS SPREAD:
A HYMN TO THE NATIVE AMERICANS AND TO THE PROPHESY OF THE WARRIORS OF THE RAINBOW WHO WILL JOIN TOGETHER TO SAVE AND RE-TEACH THE 'WAY OF THE GREAT SPIRIT'. EACH OF LYDIA COURTEILLE'S JEWELS CARRY THE SYMBOLISM OF THE NATIVE AMERICAN TRIBES

Digital image by Natalie Shau

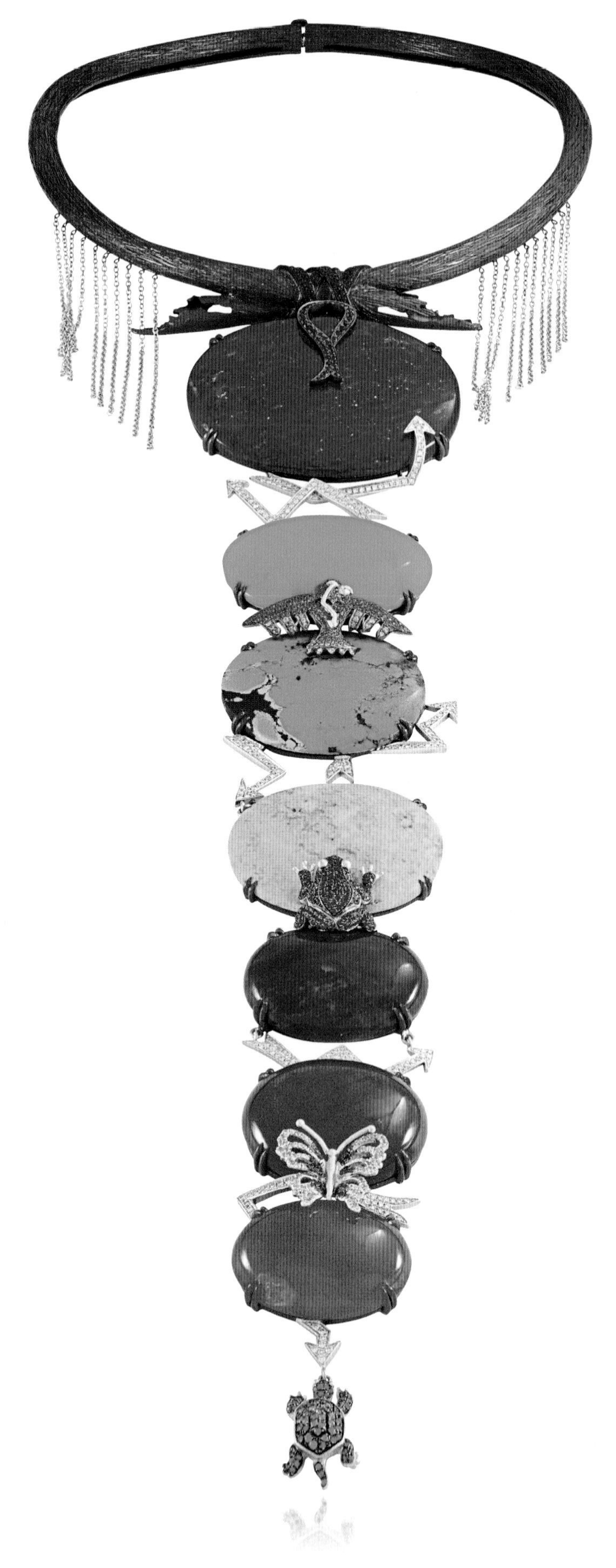

OPPOSITE PAGE:
NECKLACE – LAPIS LAZULI, TURQUOISE, GREEN TURQUOISE, YELLOW JASPER, SUGILITE, RUBY, RED CHALCEDONY, RED ENAMEL, BROWN RHODIUM-PLATED GOLD

RIGHT:
SILEX FEATHER EAR PENDANTS – CHRYSOCOLLA, TURQUOISE, SILEX ARROWHEADS, CHAMPAGNE-COLOURED DIAMOND, WHITE DIAMOND, WHITE GOLD

BELOW:
DESIGN FOR THE SILEX FEATHER EAR PENDANTS SHOWN RIGHT; GOUACHE ON CANSON PAPER
Gouache by Armelle Fontaine.

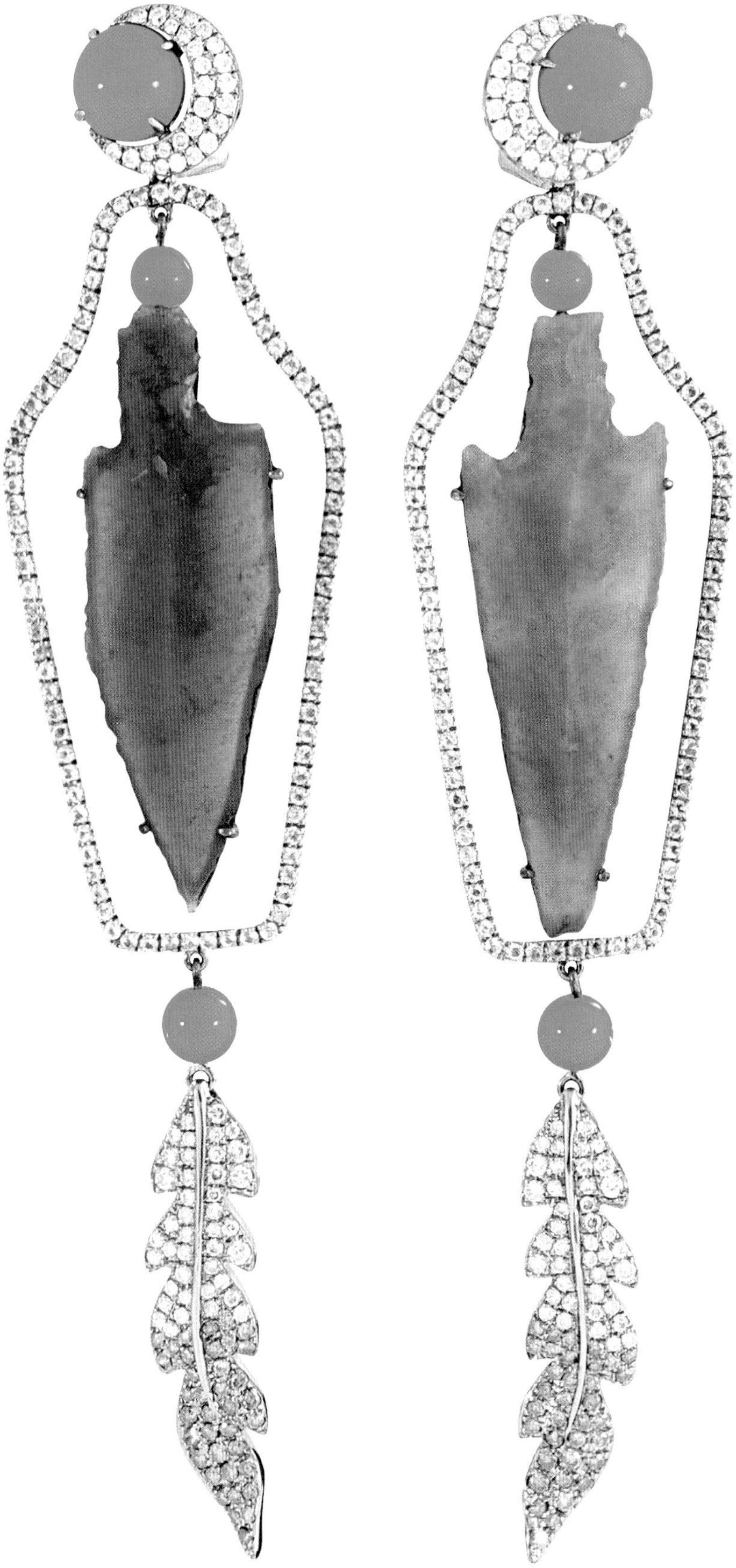

"I really had the impression that I could feel their spirits in the National Parks, at Bryce Canyon, and in Yosemite Park."

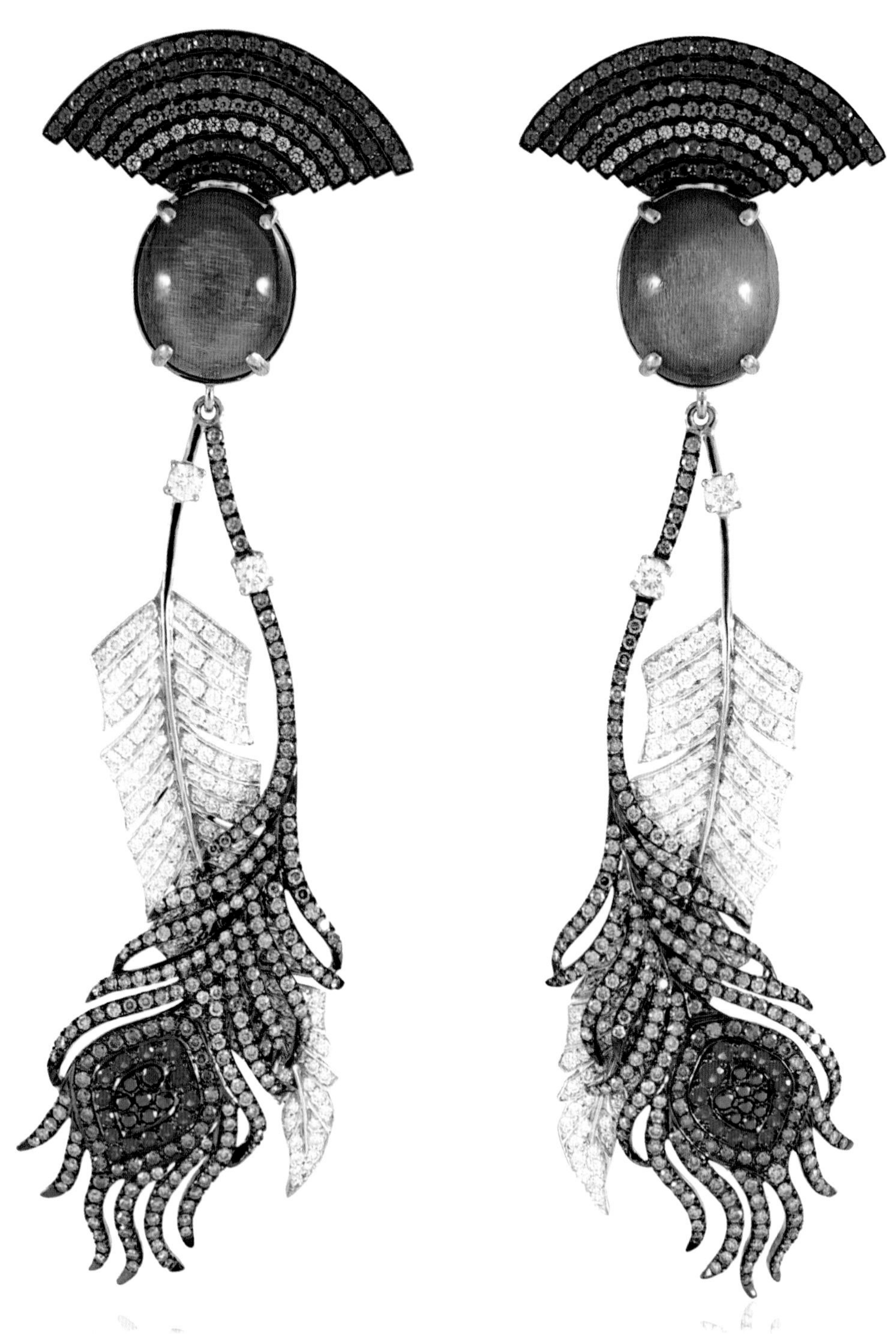

OPPOSITE PAGE:
FEATHER EAR PENDANTS – SUN STONE, MULTI-COLOURED SAPPHIRE, TSAVORITE GARNET, CHAMPAGNE-COLOURED DIAMOND, BLACK AND WHITE DIAMOND, BLACK RHODIUM-PLATED GOLD, WHITE GOLD, ROSE GOLD

ABOVE:
LIGHTNING RING – BROWN MOONSTONE, MULTI-COLOURED SAPPHIRE, AMETHYST, TSAVORITE GARNET, DIAMOND, BROWN RHODIUM-PLATED GOLD, YELLOW GOLD

HEADRESS BANGLE – CHRYSOCOLLA DRUSY WITH QUARTZ CRYSTAL,TURQUOISE, CORAL, RED SPINEL, BLUE SAPPHIRE, TSAVORITE GARNET, CHAMPAGNE-COLOURED DIAMOND, DIAMOND (YELLOW, BLACK AND WHITE), ENAMEL, BLACK RHODIUM-PLATED GOLD

QUEEN OF
SHEBA

ABOVE:
PROCESSIONAL 'MENORAH' EARRINGS – YELLOW SAPPHIRE, PERIDOT, EMERALD, TSAVORITE GARNET, BLACK RHODIUM-PLATED GOLD

PREVIOUS SPREAD:
THE QUEEN OF SHEBA LIES IN FRONT OF A BACKDROP TO THE SULPHUROUS DALLOL VOLCANIC CRATER IN THE DANAKIL DESERT. SHE WEARS JEWELS THAT HINT OF THE COVENANT OF THE ARCHANGEL GABRIEL AND THE LION OF JUDAH. LYDIA COURTEILLE USES THE ACID YELLOWS AND GREENS OF HER TOURMALINES AND PERIDOTS TO INTERPRET THE ETHIOPIAN JUDAIC AND CHRISTIAN LEGACY
Digital image by Natalie Shau

QUEEN OF SHEBA (2015)

The Queen of Sheba was born in the North of Ethiopia over 3,000 years ago, she is alluded to in most of the great religions and is mentioned in both the Muslim Koran and the Old Testament. To many in the West she is known as the Queen of Sheba. Legend tells the story of how King Solomon tricked the powerful Queen into an affair when she went to see him to assure the trade routes of Southern Arabia.

Drawing inspiration from this great mythical and biblical figure of Ethiopian and Arabian legend and by the ancient Judeo-Christian culture of Ethiopia, Lydia Courteille has created a collection that is anchored in the fertile and acid greens of the Ethiopian landscape.

Ethiopia is believed to be the home to the twelfth tribe of Israel, the Beta Israel or Falasha tribe. It is said that after the destruction of Israel by the Assyrians in 8th century BC that one of the twelve tribes of Israel, the tribe of Dan crossed the Red Sea to Ethiopia, where they continued to live and practice their religion for generations. Courteille takes her cue from this tradition to bring Judaic symbolism into her jewels to rest alongside the architecture, Christian symbols, colours and other traditions of Ethiopia, such as the Lion of Judah. The carved rock monolithic churches of Lalibela and Tigrayan are another source of inspiration for Courteille, they are hugely important sites of Christian pilgrimage in Ethiopia: the Tigray site is one of caves and churches decorated with fascinating Coptic frescos on the interior rock walls and at Lalibela, the

freestanding churches have been carved out of the rock below ground level.

Another catalyst for Courteille is the Ark of the Covenant (housing the tablets of the Ten Commandments), which according to Ethiopian tradition is housed in the Church of Our Lady Mary of Zion in Aksum. The shapes and forms of Ethiopian processional holy crosses and the Maltese cross are present and the outline shapes of religious mitres have also been used in this collection.

Courteille journeyed to Ethiopia in 2010 and the fruits of her observations have been transformed into a poetic emotional landscape of beryls, peridots, tourmalines and delicate white opals. She combines yellows with greens to represent the volcanic sulphurous pools of Dallol and the great phantasmagorical, sulphur landscapes of the Danakil desert in the North East of Ethiopia; where camel trains of salt have laboured for thousands of years.

Intrigued by the colourful umbrellas of the market places and struck by the heavy loads that women carried on their heads, Courteille also created jewels as an homage to these courageous women. The veils worn by many of the Ethiopian women, were also incorporated into her ideas.

This collection is as much about colour as it is about shapes and meaning. Inspired by the extraordinary work of the photographer Hans Silvester in the Omo Valley with its diverse tribes such as the Mursi and Kwegu tribes, Courteille draws together the essence of these very different worlds in the North and South of the country.

ECLESIASTICAL RING (VARIOUS VIEWS) – PERIDOT, YELLOW SAPPHIRE, TSAVORITE GARNET, BLACK RHODIUM-PLATED GOLD

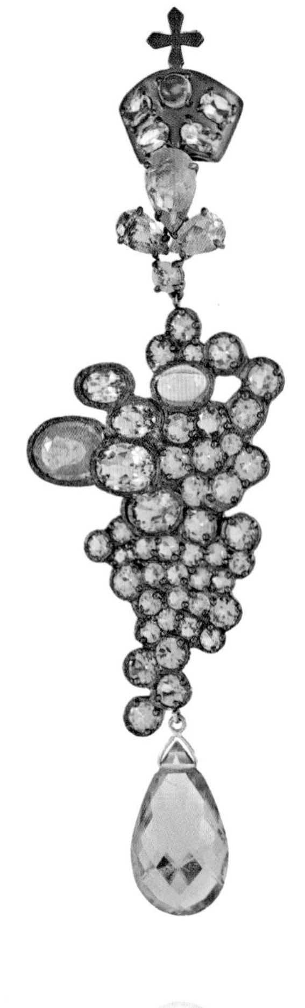
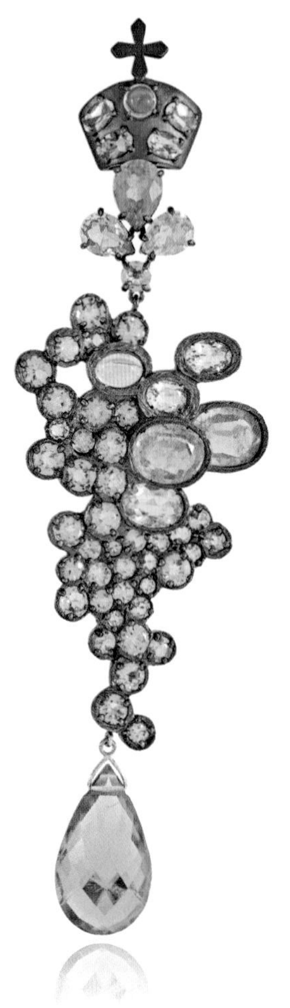

ABOVE:
MITRE PENDANT EARRINGS – YELLOW SAPPHIRE, YELLOW TOURMALINE, PERIDOT, ETHIOPIAN OPAL, EMERALD, BROWN RHODIUM-PLATED GOLD

LEFT:
TERRACED DANAKIL RING – PERIDOT, YELLOW SAPPHIRE, YELLOW TOURMALINE, TSAVORITE GARNET, OPAL, TEXTURED BROWN RHODIUM-PLATED GOLD

LEFT:
SERPENT PENDANT EARRINGS – YELLOW SAPPHIRE, YELLOW AND GREEN TOURMALINE, TSAVORITE GARNET, PERIDOT DROPS, WHITE DIAMOND, BLACK RHODIUM-PLATED GOLD

BELOW:
SULPHUR FORMATIONS AT DALLOL, DANAKIL DEPRESSION, ETHIOPIA
© imageBROKER/REX/Shutterstock
The green acid ponds of iron oxide, sulphur and salt serve as colour inspiration for Lydia Courteille

OPPOSITE PAGE:
SIMPLE ETHIOPIAN PAINTINGS ON TREE BARK REPRESENTING THE EVANGELISTS AND THE SUN

RIGHT:
'ARK ANGEL' RING – EMERALD, TSAVORITE GARNET, YELLOW TOURMALINE, YELLOW SAPPHIRE, CHAMPAGNE-COLOURED DIAMOND, BLACK RHODIUM-PLATED GOLD

BELOW:
'ARK OF THE COVENANT' RING (TOP AND SIDE VIEWS) – GREEN TOURMALINE, TSAVORITE GARNET, YELLOW SAPPHIRE, BLACK RHODIUM-PLATED GOLD
Representing the Ark of the Covenant (housing the tablets of the Ten Commandments), which according to tradition is in the Church of Our Lady Mary of Zion in Aksum.

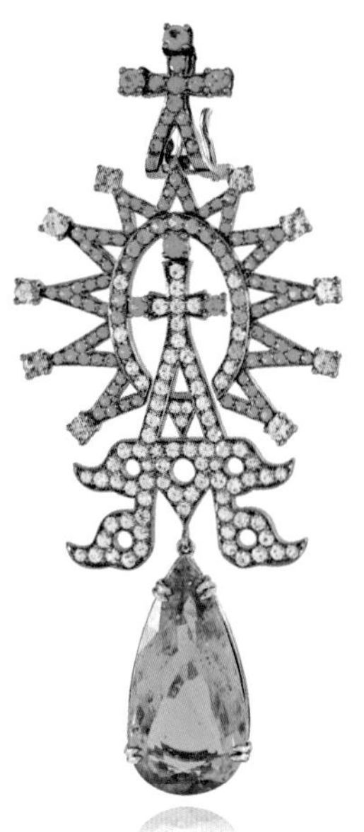
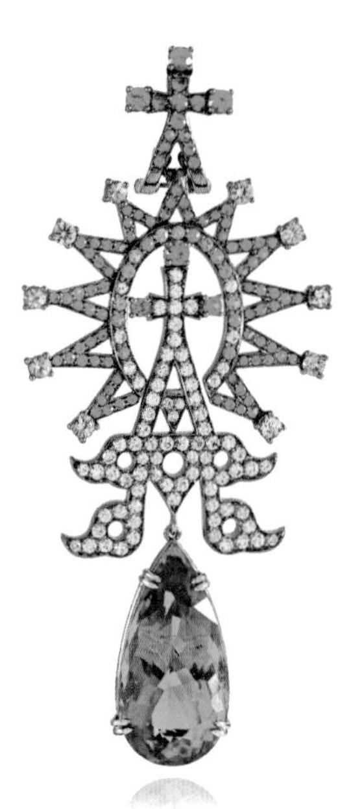
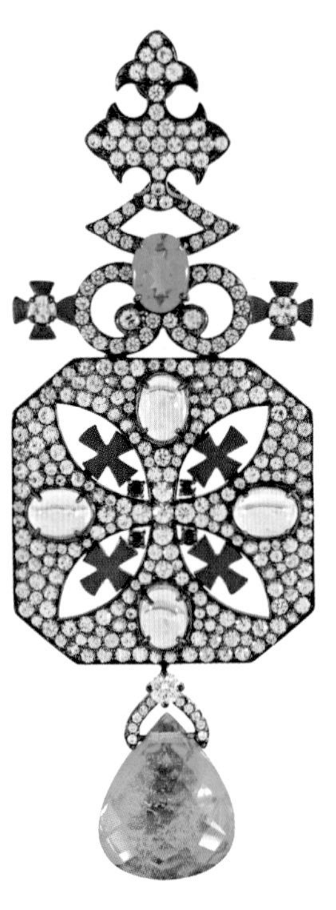

ABOVE LEFT:
PROCESSIONAL EARRINGS – PERIDOT, GREEN TOURMALINE, TSAVORITE GARNET, YELLOW SAPPHIRE, BLACK RHODIUM-PLATED GOLD

ABOVE RIGHT:
PROCESSIONAL EARRINGS – PERIDOT, OPAL, EMERALD, YELLOW SAPPHIRE, DIAMOND, BLACK RHODIUM-PLATED GOLD

RIGHT:
PROCESSIONAL RING – GREEN TOURMALINE, TSAVORITE GARNET, PERIDOT, BLACK RHODIUM-PLATED GOLD

LEFT:
YOUNG BOY FROM THE OMO VALLEY HOLDING A CHICK.
Courtesy of Hans Silvester, from his book *Natural Fashion*, published in 2009 by Thames & Hudson

BELOW:
HOMME ARBRE (TREE MAN) RING – PERIDOT, EMERALD, YELLOW TOURMALINE, TEXTURED BROWN RHODIUM-PLATED GOLD, YELLOW GOLD

CONCLUSION
GOTHIC STORY TELLING

ABOVE LEFT:
'ABYSSE' COLLECTION, SEAHORSE RING – BLACK OPAL, SAPPHIRE (PURPLE, YELLOW, PINK AND BLUE), AMETHYST, SPINEL, DIAMOND, BLACK RHODIUM-PLATED GOLD.

ABOVE RIGHT:
LION OF JUDAH RING – YELLOW SAPPHIRE, ONYX, TSAVORITE GARNET, CHAMPAGNE- AND COGNAC-COLOURED DIAMOND, BLACK RHODIUM-PLATED GOLD
The Lion of Judah is the emblem of the tribe of Juda, one of the twelve tribes of Israel. It was also used on the Ethiopian national flag until 1975.

OPPOSITE PAGE:
QUAND MÊME!

Courteille has overcome several obstacles to become such a relevant source of inspiration in the jewellery world today. Her many awards can be defined most notably by her most recent accomplishments: at the International Couture Awards in Las Vegas in 2012, she received the Couture Design Award 'Coloured Gemstone Design', and then at the Hong Kong International Jewelry Show Awards in 2013, where she won the ultimate award 'Champion of the Champions'. Both awards honoured Courteille's inventive use of coloured gemstones as well as for their rarity and quality.

In 2014 Courteille earned yet another accolade, at the AGTA Spectrum Awards, again for her imaginative and spectacular use of coloured gemstones. The sapphires were set to pick out and highlight the blues, pinks and purples in the large boulder opal at the centre of the award-winning ring.

Starting out as a jewellery expert, winning awards beginning with the award 'Talent d'Or de L'Audace' in 2008 (Golden talent for audacity and creativity), from the Comité du Luxe et Creation, Paris, Courteille has come full circle to become a judge for the Intergem Idar-Oberstein competition in October, 2015.

From symbolism to duality, Courteille plays with words; poetry; history and folk art on the one hand, and emblems and effigies as well as the cultures and beliefs of today and yesteryear on the other; they are all present to create her complex multi-layered jewels. In Lydia Courteille's treasure chest, baroque dream-like works of art await the perfect partner to take them away and with whom a new story is about to be created and told.

ACKNOWLEDGEMENTS

First and foremost, I would like to thank Liliane Schoonjans, aka Lydia Courteille, for her enthusiasm and encouragement for this book. She has been a fountain of knowledge and an inspiration.

Armelle Fontaine, Cècile Laurent and Alain Mairot for their constant support. Susannah Hecht, my editor; Sandra Pond, the book's designer; and James Smith at ACC Art Books, who have been by my side since the beginning of this adventure.

Of the many museums who made available images illustrated in the book, I would like to pick out the Richard H. Driehaus Museum, Chicago; the Dalí Museum in Saint Petersburg, Florida and the Bundesmobilienverwaltung for the Sisi Museum in the Hofburg Palace in Vienna; all have generously offered their encouragement and images for this project.

Others who kindly lent me photographs were Sotheby's Inc. New York; the commissaire-priseur Thierry Desbenoit & associés and Nadya Behmen as well as the Marquis of Salisbury at Hatfield House for the Rainbow portrait of Queen Elizabeth I. Many photographers have also been generous with their work and I would like to thank in particular Thibaut Rondoni, John Paul Pietrus and Christophe di Pascale.

I would also like to thank Veronique Mamelli at the Photographic Agency of the Réunion des Musées Nationaux-Grand Palais for her patience and help.

Juliet Weir-de La Rochefoucauld

Lydia Courteille wishes to thank:

Photography:
Guillaume Benoit
Loic Masi
Stephane Mounet
Dominique Rondoni
Thibaut Rondoni
Vogue France

Window Displays:
Christian Jacquey
Hervé Sauvage

Website:
Pascal Antoinet
Simon Elcham
Marusha Gabro
Cecile Laurent
Thibaut Rondoni
Natalie Shau
Thierry Valat

Design development and workshops:
Eric Abitbol
Antony
Samantha Arviv
Atelier IOV
Leo Bastaraud
Arda and Aylin Bora
Hervé Boudon
Jean Charles Bourgeois
Chanpen and his team
Sittijeh and Lily Chavanaves
Serge Dusaillant
Armelle Fontaine
Pauly Graveur
Avedis Kendir
Vincent Livet
Christian Obry
Pascal Sert

Collaborations and encouragement:
Alice de Boishue
Jean Pierre Brun
Edouard Brunet
Maria Doulton
Charly Jacob
Karl Lagerfeld
Lucie Lamotte
Cecile Laurent
Alain Mairot
Jean-Luc Martin du Daffoy
Musée des Arts Décoratifs, Paris

Michel Perinet
Marguerite Sam

LYDIA COURTEILLE DRESSED FOR THE GALA PERFORMANCE OF *ROMEO AND JULIET* AT THE OPÉRA PARIS, 1983

INDEX

Page numbers in **bold** refer to images and/or captions